D0982883

BF
481
.023

Oates, Wayne Edwards

Workaholics, make laziness work for you

DATE DUE

0165 00 843433 01 B 0
OATES. WAYNE EDWARDS
WORKAHOLICS. MAKE LAZINESS
(2) 1978 3 BF 481 .023

The Sidney B. Coulter Library
Onondaga Community College
Rte. 173, Onondaga Hill
Syracuse, New York 13215

A Right to Laziness Test

Instructions: Answer each of the following questions with a "Yes" or "No." If you have more than seven "Yes" answers, you really need to read this book. After you have completed the book and applied some of the suggestions, at most you should have only three "Yes" answers. At the back of the book you will find another test for your "post test."

1. Do you rise from your bed immediately upon awakening and start dressing for the day's work?
2. Do you plan your day with appointments bumper-to-bumper from beginning to end?
3. Do you get to work exceptionally early and stay at work exceptionally late?
4. Do you eat your lunch in less than fifteen minutes?
5. When you move from one place to another, do you hurry without emergency reasons?
6. Do you miss your lunch altogether and go to dinner famished, only to overeat?
7. Do you schedule breakfast meetings for work?
8. Do you schedule dinner meetings for work?
9. Do you have any half-hour periods during the day when you are completely alone?
10. Do you take a nap during the day?
11. Do you procrastinate about taking your vacation time?
12. Do you avoid discussions with your family about plans for a vacation?
13. Have you recently canceled your vacation because of work?
14. Would you like to quit work for a year's leave of absence on your own terms for the use of the year?
15. Do you have some interests of your own you would like to fulfill by retiring early?
16. Has your doctor recently told you to "slow down," get out from under some of your stress, etc., and been ignored by you?
17. Do you enjoy the fantasy of being a hobo, a beach bum, a drifter, a ne'er-do-well?
18. Do you find yourself fretting when other people do not "move at your command" or work as fast as you do?
19. Do you try to do three or four things at once?
20. Do you think that there is no limit to what you can accomplish if you will only try hard enough?
21. Do you always resent being interrupted at what you are doing?

Other books by *Wayne E. Oates*

Pastoral Care in Grief and Separation
Before You Marry Them (with Wade Rowatt)
Pastoral Counseling
The Psychology of Religion
Confessions of a Workaholic
Anxiety in Christian Experience
Where to Go for Help
When Religion Gets Sick
Seekers After a Mature Faith (with E. Glenn Hinson)
Holy Spirit and Contemporary Man
Bible and Pastoral Care
Christian Pastor
Introduction to Pastoral Counseling
Premarital Pastoral Care and Counseling
Grace Sufficient
Pastoral Counseling in Social Problems

Workaholics, Make Laziness Work for You

Wayne E. Oates, 1917-

DOUBLEDAY & COMPANY, INC.

GARDEN CITY, NEW YORK

1978

The Sidney B. Coulter Library
Onondaga Community College
Rte. 173, Onondaga Hill
Syracuse, New York 13215

The author and publisher express their appreciation to the following for permission to include excerpts from the material indicated:

American Heritage Publishing Company, Inc. for *Bigness in Business,* by Richard Townsend. Copyright © 1973 by American Heritage Publishing Company, Inc., reprinted by permission of *Horizon* (Winter 1973).

James Baldwin for "A Personal Search for a Bicentennial Candidate" (published by the Los Angeles *Times*); reprinted by permission of James Baldwin.

The *Courier-Journal* for "No Big Cheese." Copyright © 1977 by *The Courier-Journal;* reprinted with permission.

M. Evans and Company, Inc. for *Shifting Gears* by George and Nena O'Neill. Copyright © 1974 by Nena O'Neill and George O'Neill; reprinted by permission of the publishers, M. Evans and Company, Inc., New York, N.Y. 10017.

The Florida *Times Union* for material taken from their January 15, 1977, issue; reprinted by permission of the Florida *Times Union.*

W. H. Freeman and Company for "The Pathology of Boredom" by Woodbern Heron (published by the *Scientific American* in January 1957); reprinted by permission of W. H. Freeman and Company.

Grove Press for *The Autobiography of Malcolm X.* Copyright © 1964 by Alex Haley and Malcolm X. Copyright © 1965 by Alex Haley and Betty Shabazz. Reprinted by permission of Grove Press, Inc.

The Louisville *Times* for "A Lesson from Sandburg" by Ralph McGill (January 18, 1966); reprinted by permission of the Louisville *Times.*

Lyle Stuart, Inc. for *The Great Quotations* compiled by George Seldes. Copyright © 1960, 1966 by George Seldes. Reprinted by arrangement with Lyle Stuart.

William Morrow and Company, Inc. for material adapted and reprinted by permission from *The Peter Principle* by Laurence J. Peter & Raymond Hull. Copyright © 1969 by William Morrow and Company, Inc.

W. W. Norton & Company, Inc., or *The Psychiatric Interview* by Harry S. Sullivan. Copyright © 1954 by the William Alanson White Psychiatric Foundation.

The Twentieth Century Fund for *Of Time, Work and Leisure* by Sebastian deGrazia. Copyright © 1962 by the Twentieth Century Fund, New York.

ISBN: 0-385-12977-7
Library of Congress Catalog Card Number 77–80906

Copyright © 1978 by Wayne E. Oates
ALL RIGHTS RESERVED
PRINTED IN THE UNITED STATES OF AMERICA
FIRST EDITION

To
Henlee Barnette, Th.D.
My fellow slave for
forty years

Acknowledgments

For the encouragement and support of Doubleday & Company in projecting this book with me and giving me the advice and counsel of their staff, I am deeply indebted. I am especially appreciative of the work of Randall Greene, who has followed each step of the writing of this book with creative suggestions, steady reassurance, and a genuine personal friendship. Authors who have such comradeship of a publishing staff are fortunate indeed, and my own continuing education has been enriched as I have collaborated with them.

For my colleagues in the Kentucky Psychiatric Association and in the Louisville Conversation Club who permitted me to "try out" some of these ideas in conversation with them, I am especially indebted and grateful. They are a challenging company with whom to work and think. For my students who have listened and queried me about these ideas, I am especially appreciative. The Department of Psychiatry and Behavioral Sciences administrative officer, Miss Nancy Brown, and her staff of secretaries have been unusually helpful in getting the manuscript into its present form. I am especially indebted to Mrs. Bonnie Lakes and Miss Betty Tracy for their help.

Contents

Workaholics,
Make Laziness
Work for You

CHAPTER 1

The Importance of
Being Lazy

E ach one of us is as lazy as we have the courage to be. In a world of competition, productivity, status seeking, and work addiction, to be lazy is to be despised by others and often by ourselves. "Lazy" is an often-used four-letter word for people who exasperate us, wear out our patience, and defy our understanding. Laziness by definition is the disinclination to work, to exertion; the aversion to labor; indolence, idleness, sloth, or in slang, "goofing off." Therefore, it takes real courage, brass, *chutzpa*, or nerve to be lazy by deliberate choice. Yet the contempt of a workaholic, like me, for instance, for the lazy person *may* be the "sidelong glance of his or her envy." After a sigh, one says, "How does he/she get away with being so lazy? How come I never get such preferential treatment, such soft assignments?"

For example, as I had finished the above paragraph, the telephone rang. A public school teacher whom I have known as a friend of the family called. Today has been locked in a heavy snowstorm and very cold temperatures. No one in our town has been able to get to work because of the impassable roads. My friend said that Christmas holidays had been preceded by a teachers' strike of two weeks. During Christmas holidays she had spent a ten-day vacation in Hawaii. Now the snows have prevented schools from operating for three of the five days since the holidays. She said that she had come to the point that she felt horribly guilty in being as *purposely inactive* as she was. She called her principal at the school to see if there was any work that she could do at the school, even though school is officially closed. She says that neither she nor her husband has ever been used to this much legitimate idleness. For her it is taking *effort* to do nothing—to be lazy, in short. She and her husband have successfully raised and educated five sons. They are burden-bearers in their community. They have earned *the right to be lazy*. This right is not an inalienable right from birth by reason of our humanity. This right is one that we earn. Therefore, this book is addressed to folks like my friends whom I have just described. It is not an encouragement to free-loaders, malingerers, parasites, and people who have never worked enough to have anything with which to contrast and appreciate laziness. The book is addressed to the driven ones, the work-addicted ones, the people who have *earned* the right to be lazy. Yet something keeps them from cashing in on this benefit. I am one of them. You may be one of us. Look on me as "reading you your rights."

The Right to Be Lazy

The idea of laziness as a right is not new. Karl Marx died in 1883. That year his son-in-law, Paul La Fargue, wrote an essay entitled in French, *La Droit À la Paresse*. It was translated into German under the title, *Das Recht Auf Faulheit*. In both languages, then, the word for "laziness" was used. LaFargue opposed his father-in-law's economic determinism and idolatry of work. He hoped that machines could be invented to take over all the slave functions of man and be "labor-saving" devices. Thus men and women could be freed to enjoy living as well as to be responsible for making a living. Men and women would be free to enjoy each other, the arts, and the natural wonders of the earth. People generally would be lifted from the level of drudgery to the enjoyment of life for the sake of living. Thus, leisure, or earned laziness, would not be the sole right of the so-called "leisure classes." It would be within the reach of all men and women.

This angle of vision sees invention as the cleverness of essentially lazy people, i.e., people who are looking for an easier, less-burdensome way of doing the work of the world. The wheel became the invention of a person somewhere in the distant past who preferred to ride rather than to walk. Household appliances, such as washers, dryers, vacuum cleaners, self-cleaning ovens, etc. ease the burden of housekeeping. They originated in the mind of someone who was attuned to the need for leisure, the right to be lazy when it comes to the more vexatious tasks. When we see the liberation, not of affluent classes, but of the poverty level and oppressed minorities such as Chicanos, blacks, and Puerto Ricans—who would otherwise be doing these tasks by hand—then we see something of what Paul LaFargue was talking about over a century ago. Unskilled persons are put into the situation of having to learn a more satisfying and less-drudging kind of work. The woman who previously employed a maid at ruthlessly low wages in order to be "freed" of these tasks now uses "labor-saving" household appliances.

Yet, when we push further the relation of the inventive mind to laziness, we see how affluent persons are caught in the web of our own access to these inventions' use. They simply give us the opportunity to add more work to our week. For example, I can recall one of the most meaningful trips I ever took. I was asked to come to Shamokin, Pennsylvania, to deliver some lectures. It was 1954. At that time we had good train service. I rode the train. I got on the train in the late afternoon in my home city. I ate a leisurely dinner in the dining car. I then returned to a small Pullman roomette. I read a fine book until bedtime. I then retired to awaken the next morning in southwestern Pennsylvania. I dressed and went to breakfast. The Susquehanna River followed alongside the train's right of way as we rode along. Then, I returned to my roomette and finished reading my book. I arrived, refreshed and renewed, in the early afternoon of the next day after I had left home. The return trip was a similar treat of leisurely contemplation.

Today, if I were to make a similar trip, I would work at my tasks at home ten of the twenty-four hours it took me to make the trip by train. Then I would take a plane and make the trip in three more of those hours. I would leave the city and return to my home in time to work ten more of the hours here at home that I would have otherwise spent traveling by train. Thus, I use the time saved by additional speed of the plane simply to add to my work week and my exhaustion. Planes deprive me of the lazy leisure of the train trip. The wisdom of some other person's invention becomes the occasion of my own voluntary deprivation of my right to laziness.

This coming weekend, I am going to do something about this. I have to speak in Daytona Beach, Florida. I plan to get out of this snow a day early and stay a day late in Daytona Beach. It is not warm enough there to enjoy the sunshine of 80° temperature, but is much warmer than the 10° below zero we will have here tonight. I am imagining that I am using the train schedule, while all the while I am using the invention of the plane. I will exercise my right to leisurely travel by getting at least one full day watching the ocean and walking on the beach.

The crunch of daily decision making comes when you and I choose to make technology do a few things *for* us, for a change, rather than letting technology do so much *to* us. The inventive mind produces aerodynamic, electronic, and chemical servants to ease and smooth the way for men and women. In turn, you and I do not allow them to work for us. They make you and me ten times more a slave than our parents and grandparents did without these "labor-saving" devices. To make such choices implies that you have worked hard enough, long enough, and responsibly enough to have a *range* of choice as to how you will live your life. The exercise of the right to laziness is a result of having created this range of choice by prior effort. Yet the very prior effort implies that you have had the right to work, the freedom to work, the opportunity to work, and the discipline to work as a precondition of the exercise of the right to laziness. Not all persons, as you will see in the latter portion of this book, have had this right and freedom and opportunity to work. Yet, they are seen and experienced as being lazy to such an extent that inaction is both a tool for anger and a foil for fear. Since you were a child, idleness in any form has been described as a sort of forge of evil. Laziness becomes incendiary both emotionally and sociopolitically when it does not exist in tension with work as a basis of comparison and contrast. Work becomes slavery when it does not exist in comparison and tension with the right to laziness.

The Principle of Laziness by "Dosage"

The indispensability of sleep is a mysterious reality that suggests that resting *from* labor, resting *in* one's work, implies a prior condition of activity, action, productivity, work. If you are a healthy person, you can work only so long without sleep; you can sleep only so long without a reasonable dosage of working activity. Hence, I suggest that laziness be a prescription with accurate dosage for your age, weight, height, etc.—especially your age. Too much laziness is like too much of any other prescription. Just because 100 mgs. of Elavil will, if taken at the right times in the twenty-four-hour cycle, aid in combating a severe depression, does not mean that a ten-day's dosage of Elavil taken all at once will work ten times as fast and do ten times as much good. People die that way, especially if they also take alcohol at the same time. The principle of dosage must be observed.

"Dosage" has two meanings in our language. Both meanings are useful in understanding the proper exercise of the right to laziness. The first meaning refers to the restoration or maintenance of the balance or homeostasis of the body through medication. Ordinarily, the "wisdom of the body", i.e., the biochemistry and physiology of the body, collaborates in such a way that the balance or homeostasis is maintained naturally. When this does not happen and the person develops imbalances, medications are introduced to restore that balance. If this is a chronic deficiency of the body, then medications are introduced to maintain that balance. The correct dosage is related to that restoration and/or maintenance of the balance, the homeostasis. Medications can, therefore, be taken on a daily basis, at stated intervals, and in differing quantities. *Quantities differ in four levels: first, homeopathic or the barest minimum quantity; second, the moderate dosage; third, the maximum dosage; fourth, the lethal dosage, i.e., the amount that will produce death.*

When you apply the analogy of dosage to the exercise of laziness, you get some interesting guidelines for the beneficence and lethality of laziness. You have often heard the adage that "work never killed anyone." You can also say that total inactivity *has* killed many people. With others whom it has not killed, it has reduced to the death of the spirit or *élan vital* of the person. Yet, even those others have never permitted themselves to do nothing, to have any leisure, to goof off, to be lazy. They have forced themselves into exhaustion, depression, cardiovascular disorders, excessive eating in order to maintain energy, and all manner of imbalances of the human life. Then, there are those persons who have never committed themselves to any kind of work. They may be financially secure with inheritances of money and property. Some gradually slide into a hobo existence and/or what psychiatrists readily identify as simple schizophrenia. They absorb lethal doses of inactivity, laziness, torpidness of life. Their lethargy kills their relationships to persons, destroys their creative involvement in the ongoingness of life, and leaves them at a sort of vegetative level of existence.

Consequently, rest, leisure, laziness is necessary for the maintenance, sustenance and renewal of the balanced life. Yet it must come in individually prescribed, carefully matched doses, depending upon a careful study of your and my work-play, play-rest, rhythms. A hobo personality will need only homeopathic doses of laziness. A young person who is running a full-time job and going to school three nights a week will need short intervals of laziness "b.i.d., t.i.d., or q.i.d.," which, being translated, means twice a day, three times a day, or four times a day. A successful business or professional person may need maximum doses of laziness up to and including two full days a week. A workaholic like myself may suffer withdrawal symptoms from work if pushed beyond a week's vacation at a time. If you are like me, you might need to take several short vacations in the course of a year instead of one long vacation of a month or two months at a time. In order to sustain the balance of your organism, you may need the regular supervision of a spiritual director. Such a spiritual director can insist upon reminding you and even order such dosages of laziness.

Homeopathic Doses of Laziness

Now why go into all this tilting of windmills about "dosage" from a prescriptive point of view? The second meaning of dosage helps us to see that "why's" answer. A classical and less well-known meaning of the word dosage is "the process of adding some ingredient, as to wine, to give it flavor, character, and strength." For example, in the middle 1750s Madeira shippers scientifically added brandy to some of their wines for the purpose of adding flavor, character, and strength. Also, pink champagne is made by adding a little red wine. Dryness or sweetness are opposites in proportion to the addition of small amounts of syrup. Trivial amounts are added for ascending orders of sweetness, i.e., extra dry, *sec, demi-sec,* and *doux*.

Let this be another analogy for understanding the place of laziness in the life of "flavor, character, strength." One of the most-often-said things about a responsible, hard-working professional or business person like yourself is that you are "busy," "too busy," "in a hurry," "running late," etc. These are so many stock-in-trade comments that you begin to *think this way about yourself*. Yet this self-image sustains your *place* among your peers. You raise the *price* of your time this way. You put yourself on the market of supply-and-demand for your services. Something needs to be added to your life to give it flavor, character and strength. What is it? It is deliberately taken time, deliberate casualness, laziness, if you will permit the word. Nonchalance, i.e., to be casual, indifferent to hurry, to have no feeling for this glorified image of "busyness," is the flavor, character, and strength that is needed in your life when laziness is added. Persons who know you as a "busy character" are caught off guard with a surprising joy that causes them to say, "He [she] gets a lot done but always has time for me."

Such deliberate freedom from frenzied hurry is the antithesis of "the White Rabbit Syndrome." You will remember the White Rabbit from Lewis Carroll's *Alice in Wonderland* (or Walt Disney's animated version of it). He was controlled by a huge watch in his waistcoat pocket and continually saying at every contact with others, "I am late I am late, for a very important date." When it *always* is someone else that matters more, no one matters really. The captured moments of lazy leisure in relation to time can be focused in wholehearted attention on persons whom you meet. These are minuscules of lazy parentheses in human existence when one other person becomes totally significant to you.

The story is told by residents of Princeton, New Jersey, about the mother whose nine-year-old daughter came home from school one day and told her mother that she already had her arithmetic lessons for the next day prepared. The mother asked how she had been able to do this when she had had so much trouble with arithmetic on other days. She said that she had met a kind old man sitting on a bench on the street near the bus stop. He had asked her if she liked mathematics. She had told him she was having trouble with numbers. He then carefully explained her lesson to her and showed her how easy it was for her to get the hang of doing arithmetic. The mother was somewhat concerned about her daughter being in conversation with a stranger. She investigated and found out that this old man was Albert Einstein! Do you have time to talk with a child? Or are they simply additions to an exploding population? Statistics?

I find patients in hospital beds, corridors, and lounge rooms who have had no one to slow down long enough to talk with them about anything except their illness. This is especially true of mentally ill persons who are often not bedfast. They long to talk with someone who is not so tightly wrapped up in his or her responsibility to "treat" the patient that he or she cannot—for a little while, at least—see them as ordinary human beings and not as a collection of symptoms and reactions to medications. A patient will stop me, as one did, and want to show me the pictures of his children. I just happen to have pictures of my sons and my granddaughter. We share our feelings about our families. Such a breathing time in the middle of the battle against disease and the search for health amounted to our putting down our burdens long enough to "kill a little time" together doing nothing but that which came naturally.

These are minimum, almost homeopathic, doses of laziness. You can say you are too busy, you are late for a very important date, your important presence and attention is so special that it can only be given *elsewhere* and never here and now. The spur of the moment is a drop of laziness that belongs to us all as an earned right. All you have to do is take it. You do not have to ask for it. It is offered to you by those around you. In moments of unexpected interruption it literally saves you from your "breakneck" speeds.

Moderate Doses of Laziness

If you harshly condemn the unrestrained and inordinate laziness of the gold-brickers, free-loaders, rip-off artists, and lead-butts of our society, you are wise to consider yourself, lest you are being tempted by the same excesses. The psychiatric estimate of this kind of behavior is called a "reaction-formation." This is a form of defense against urges of mine and yours that are unacceptable. It is our own insecurity protest that is constantly being threatened by its opposite behaviors when you and I see those behaviors in others, especially. On this basis, then, you might think of the unreconstructed workaholics as persons who are unable to absorb moderate doses of inactivity, rest, leisure, and/or laziness because of our own temptation to those excesses in others. Their excess drives you and me away from moderation. As a driven and compulsive worker, then, may you be struggling against the fantasy of being a beach bum! Your only recovery is in moderate doses of laziness taken on a well-modulated schedule.

The combined work-vacation. One major dose of laziness is that of taking work assignments because you *want* to take them and not because you feel you *ought* to take them for some external reason. Then add several days after or before the assignment to take advantage of its vacation advantages. This is such a common practice that conventions are planned with this in mind. I prefer to suggest that one take the vacation *after* the work so you will not be preoccupied with the work. In fact, you are cashing in on your right to laziness. Obviously, the context of this suggestion points toward the person having the kind of work in which moderate amounts of travel are a part of the job.

The Long Weekend Without Getting Drunk or Getting a Cold

One of the substitute gains of compulsive drinking is that the worker who has the Monday morning hangover gets a day off from work. When a person's stress system has "gotten to him/her" to such an extent that he/she hurts in one place, he/she needs to divert. By that, one would mean to do something different, shift to another assignment in one's work, etc. However, when a person's stress has produced pain all over him/her, then he/she should get total bed rest. The person who is prone to drink too much and be forced to take off from work does much better simply to take a long weekend without getting drunk. Take off Friday or Monday and either get some diverting activity in, such as brief trip to a nearby place of recreation and rest, or simply staying in bed for the whole weekend except for meals and the bathroom.

Those people who do not drink may have to rely on the common cold to create the kind of "permission" to be lazy for seventy-two hours. I like the idea of sensing when a cold is *about* to take over. The unexplainable headache, the slight nausea, the stuffiness of the nose, the raspiness of the throat . . . these premonitory symptoms alert me to the fact that a cold is on the way. Purposeful laziness in advance is a delightful way of "beating the system" of a common cold. You may think that this is a callous way to go, a calculating way to wring your rights out of your employer while you loll back into laziness. To the contrary, what a favor you are doing the rest of the employees! You do not take a cold to work with you and infect the whole crowd with it. The employer's least interest are cared for, too. You may take *one* day off to prevent an upper respiratory infection. If you let the illness force you down, you may have to lose several days' work. Admit it! Did you not enjoy staying in bed and reading a good book the last time you had a cold? Why not deliberately stay in bed to stave off a cold? Frankly admit that you are goofing off in order not to hazard the side effects of antibiotics as well as the impact of influenza? In these days of woman's liberation, I am putting in a word for "sick days" for men once a month whether they are sick or not. It does not seem right in the days of equal rights for men to be denied one day a month's sick leave just because men don't menstruate.

Moderate doses of laziness will do much to aid the morale of the working force. It is unjust for a few people in an organization to pre-empt *all* the laziness in the place. Laziness that is earned is laziness that should be equalized and calibrated so that all the work force gets their part. Why should you not get your part of the lion's share?

Maximum Doses of Laziness

Maximum doses of laziness consist of such things as a month's vacation, extended leave with pay, and retirement. More attention is to be paid to these in later chapters of this book. However, it is important to say here that the toxicity level of laziness differs from one person to another. Some people can effectively take a whole month of vacation at once. Others suffer the rigors of anxiety, the irritability of the depressed, and the preoccupation of the "spaced out" on a vacation. This much of "not-doing" makes them eat more, sleep fitfully, and count the passing of time as if they had metronomes in the backs of their heads.

Furthermore, a serious consideration of the importance of being lazy and the exercise of the right to laziness is a prerequisite to the state of being retired. This maximum, culturally sanctioned, and legally enforced dose of laziness is lethal to some people. Retirement is legally prescribed in the pharmacopoeia of work in this land of ours. Yet it is fought against and considered a dirty word. Retirement is taken as a "sentence" rather than as an opportunity by a considerable portion of the population. In fact, the laws are so written that a man who married somewhat late in life and/or married a woman much younger than himself cannot afford to retire if they become parents. Thus, the right to the leisure implicit in the Social Security system is denied many persons on this and innumerable other counts.

For many, then, the maximum dosages of laziness allowed by law can be lethal or unavailable to large segments of our population.

Lethal Dosages of Laziness

In the early life of the State Churches, such as Catholicism, Lutheranism, and Anglicanism, certain positions were available to people they employed. They were called sinecure positions. Literally the term meant in the beginning that these positions were positions in which the person did not have any responsibility for the "cure of souls," or pastoral care. With the passage of time and the secularization of the word, however, the term came to mean that the person is given a job in which there are few if any duties, little if any responsibility, work, or service. The person was paid, held the position, but did not work.

I first recall seeing this kind of job when I was a page in the United States Senate. Certain senators would appoint members of their family to a position for which that person was paid for holding a position. However, they did no work for that money. On occasion, another person, not related to the particular senator, would perform the duties of work in order to keep his or her own job. Usually these duties were done as overtime on the part of the patronage employee. I do not know whether this kind of practice still prevails, but I was an eyewitness to it in 1933.

However, I am convinced that to hold such a job with no duties is a lethal dose of laziness. The person's whole integrity is at stake. Recently, in a Florida newspaper, I read the account of a man named Ben Aronson, age fifty-six, who remained as a civil service employee on the state payroll of Illinois. He sued the government twice for attempting to lay him off from his job. Both times he won. However, they told him that whereas he would be paid a monthly salary of $1,730 a month, he would have no duties. The phone was removed from his office and the mail was cut off. Other persons were advised not to converse with him, he said. He knew how to run the whole department but was not allowed to do anything.

This much of doing nothing ravaged his health. He said, "The pressure of not working when I wanted got to me. I collapsed with internal bleeding. . . . I may have to have heart surgery. Between vacation time and sick time I have four weeks off. My doctor says I can't return to work in my condition." (*Florida Times-Union,* Jacksonville, Saturday, January 15, 1977, p. A-3.)

The paradox of work and laziness emerges vividly in this incident. The monotony and boredom of enforced laziness is indeed toxic. As Woodburn Heron said after having conducted a laboratory experiment to obtain information on how human beings react in situations where nothing at all was happening, "prolonged exposure to a monotonous environment . . . has deleterious effects. The individual's thinking is impaired; his visual perception becomes disturbed; he suffers from hallucinations; his brain-wave pattern changes." He observes that the normal functioning of the brain depends upon arousal reactions. He says that "a changing sensory environment seems essential for human beings. Without it the brain ceases to function in an adequate way, and abnormalities of behavior develop . . . variety is not the spice of life; it is the very stuff of it." ("The Pathology of Boredom," *Scientific American,* January, 1957, p. 52–56.)

The toxicity levels of both work and laziness exist in tension with each other. Either work or laziness can be antidotes for a wide variety of human conditions of suffering. The antidote powers of laziness when exercised as an earned right have not been assessed to any appreciable degree.

Laziness as an Antidote

Human beings quickly hasten to the drugstore with this or that prescription for the infections and imbalances of their lives. At times they are armed with physicians' prescriptions.

At others they are prompted and pushed by the latest television advertisement for this or that patent over-the-counter medication.

Close attention to your and my *ways of life* may reveal that we are seeking a substance of some kind or other that will relieve us of the necessity of thinking and doing something about our way of life. Scrutiny of the ways of life of many persons in addition to my own way of life has taught me that exercising the right to laziness is an *antidote* for many of these catawampus imbalances in our lives that make the taste of life like that of ashes. In several ways, the exercise of the right to laziness can indeed correct the imbalances in our own personal lives and even point toward public health measures.

An Antidote for Careless Work

"Haste makes waste" is the order of the day in much of the work done by us as Americans. Pride of product is sacrificed for quantity of production. In the sphere of writing, hack work is that of grinding out a certain amount of copy each day in order to get paid for it. The very meaning of the word "scholar" suggests the opposite kind of writing, namely, the kind of writing in which a leisurely reflection, a process of the slow and lazy maturation of thought, and the right to spend a considerable amount of time simply staring out the window in reverie. The word "scholar" comes from the Greek word σχολή meaning leisure, rest, ease. The contemporary rat race of the typical university, law school, medical school, etc. operates upon the assumption of mass production. Term papers are "ground out," "cranked out," "thrown together" in order to meet end-of-semester deadlines. The educational process is evaluated in terms of the amount of money that can be brought in by a given curriculum, degree program, or the use of different kinds of lengths of school terms. At a certain crucial point the professor-student relationship becomes critical. Objectives silently shift from actually learning to simply "getting through" the required data and getting out of the place. The subtle connection of money in the business management of the school to a degree will make one think too often of the analogy of prostitution of the learning relationships.

Erik Erikson has wisely called attention to the wisdom of a psycho-social moratorium from the rat races of achievement-in-a-hurry as a necessary antidote to such rat races as I have described above. Selective permissiveness on the part of society and "provocative playfulness" on the part of youth provide a new perspective, a clearer sense of purpose, and fresh appreciation of devotion to a duty that is uniquely ours and can be the end result of such a time of moratorium. He notes that patienthood and delinquency often are the results of nature's demanding this moratorium. Sometimes a hitch in military service serves this end.

I know a very successful physician who is a specialist in hematology. He persistently refused to work in college when his father was paying his way. He goofed off and flunked out of two or three colleges. Then he went into the Navy. He had many free hours on board ship. He could get his work done quickly and have time to think and study. He became interested in nuclear physics in his work. This led to an interest in biochemistry. From there he became interested in medicine. Upon leaving the Navy, he enrolled in college of his own accord. He went carefully through the basic sciences and on to medical school with excellent grades. He attributes much of the change to the times of leisurely reflection while at sea.

To apply the principle of leisureliness to the food and cooking field, one can only note that America is addicted to "fast foods" and "instant" types of meals. This is reminiscent of the comment of Duke Ellington, the great jazz musician. He said on his next to last birthday that he used to give thanks for food, because food was so hard to get. Later, however, he gave thanks for the time in which to eat the food—to do so unhurriedly. Oh, for the siesta after lunch!

Similarly, the production of clothes and machineries presents the carelessness of haste making waste. When a Vega Chevrolet can be produced each minute of an assembly-line operation, both the assembly-line workers and the persons who buy the cars have cause to ask for at least some minimum doses of lazy leisureliness in the production of the car. Also, when an automobile dealer's sales force will push a customer into a sale of a car and be calculating the interest on his or her monthly payments within the short scope of ten minutes, a customer has a right to refuse to sign anything. A generous amount of lazy nonchalance might even cause salesmen to realize that customers are people.

An Antidote to Trying Too Hard

The football team that is repeatedly offsides is trying too hard. Penalties result. The swimmer who is trying too hard causes the water to become his or her enemy. The collaboration of mankind with the elements in farming, in navigation at sea or in the air, or in coping with rivers, freezing temperatures, etc. constantly confronts us with our tendency to "try too hard."

Have you ever sought to get the checkbook to balance and it would not come right? The more you worked at it the worse it got. You worked and worked and worked until your efforts were past the point of diminishing returns. Then you became disgusted with the effort. You went away for a night's rest, a game of tennis, or an afternoon walk. When you got back to the checkbook, suddenly without effort on your part the balance came right and the errors were easily spotted.

Moderate doses of laziness are an antidote for fanatic effort. As you have heard, a fanatic is a person who has lost his or her sense of direction and has redoubled the effort. He is different from the man of whom I heard recently who lived to be a hundred. The centenarian said that the secret of his long life was that he learned very early to know when to give up. He said that many people keep on flailing away vainly at tasks that never should be accomplished anyhow and trying too hard to succeed at tasks that are pointless if accomplished.

An Antidote for Greed

Laziness can be an antidote for the sin of greed. The greedy person wants it *all*. The reason he overworks and never takes a long deep breath of relaxation, much less indulges in the earned right to laziness, is that he cannot forego the money, the prestige, the applause, or the trophies involved in work addiction. The work addict cannot forego running two and three jobs because he wants to build up a surplus for the mythical rainy day. Bracing themselves against retirement, workaholics may have *four* different retirement plans! Then when retirement comes they may not want to retire because that means a cut in income, even though they have retirement plans that equal their salaries.

A re-examination of laziness by a greedy workaholic will prompt a reappraisal of what a person really needs. Mencius, in 371 B.C., said in his Oriental wisdom: "To nourish the heart there is nothing than to make the desires few."

This wisdom brings back to me the story of Portie Tipton. My wife and I spent a night in his home as his guests. About nine o'clock in the evening, as we sat before the open fire, he suddenly said, "Doctor Oates, are you and Mrs. Oates feeling well?" We both said, that we felt quite well. He said, "Well, good. I'm not going to sit up with you. I'm going to bed. I only sit up with sick people!" Then he added, "If there is anything you can see that you need, it is yours. If you can't find what you need, call us and we will help you look for it. If we don't have it, we can teach you how to get along without it." Yet for you and me this is easier to say than to do.

We could have more time for leisure and the enrichment of life if we had someone to teach and encourage us to get along without half the stuff we think we need. But then we would have to learn how to use that leisure.

CHAPTER 2

Creative Laziness

T he exercise of the right to laziness is equally as dangerous as it is helpful. The same thing tends to be true of any human right, any therapeutic agent. Therefore, the creative uses of laziness are the side of the paradox I wish to pursue in this chapter. I pause and think about the sentence which I have just written. The humor of the thing hits me hard. Note: You and I are to *pursue* the creative uses of laziness! Here we are running like mad to pursue how to go about being lazy!

An event happened to me in the airport of Birmingham, Alabama. I had been dropped off at the airport by my hosts just at the time of the departure of my scheduled plane. The desk clerk said that if I would run I could make it. So I ran pell-mell down the concourse to catch my plane. I whizzed past two men carrying small cases in their hands. They were leisurely and casually walking along. One of them called to me, "Mister, there is no need for you to run like that. You need not be in such a hurry." Having gotten this double message—run and don't run—I said, "Why?" The man answered, "Because we're the pilots of your flight! You can't leave until we do anyway."

Their timely wisdom rebukes me as I write a sentence about "pursuing" creative uses of laziness. Simply, then, join me in a lackadaisical amble. Let us leisurely look at some creative ways of being lazy.

To Offset the Futility of Overproduction

When you listen to a concert pianist in a great audience that is deeply pleased with the pianist's performance, the customary thing to do is to applaud and cry "Encore!" or "More! More!" Or, take the child's game with an adult. The adult does something that brings especial glee to the child. Then the child repeatedly says, "Do it again!" until the adult is exhausted. In a sense, that is what the American way of life in work is constantly saying to you about your work: "Encore! More! More! Do it again!" Even in telling funny stories, we get into a rhythm: "Can you top this one?" Can you outcompete your neighbor? Worse than that, can you outdo *yourself*?

When you apply this theme to your work and encircle your working days, weeks, and months with it, your hard-earned right to laziness working for you is signed away. You are at best an indentured servant to work, and at worst you are a slave. The time to quit is when they are still saying "More!" But do we know that when it comes to producing goods, earning money, expanding our product, looking for bigger and better worlds to conquer? We do not. The need for more and more goods imperializes our attitudes. Goods cost more and more money. More money entails more and more taxes. All of it calls for more and more moonlighting, more and more work.

Saturday is a good day to do your own observation of this. If you live in or near a reasonably large town, note how many new shopping centers have been finished since you ever had a day free to visit them. Notice how many more freeways are opened up. Notice that the economic pulse of the nation seems to be in how many cars are sold. Notice how the trash-packer is the latest thing that you are *supposed* to buy. It will help you pack more compactly the obsolescent and often unneeded junk you bought. Remember the last time you were able to squiggle a day free to go get depressed at the way credit cards enable people to draw on the future to buy more and more things. One of the cores of the motivation of this behavior is described well as follows: A credit card is the greatest invention since the wheel. It is able to convert thrift into greed instantly and make it possible for all of us to buy things we don't need, with money we don't have to impress people we don't like. Overproduction could not run as rampant if we did not have so many encouragements, inducements, and seductions to overspend.

Therefore, one way to exercise our right to laziness is to pay cash for what you buy. Another way is to buy only what you really need. Another is to make major purchases only after a month's reflection. Make do. Think through. Gather facts. Discuss with those whom you love and respect. Yet all this is paddling upstream in the culture in which we live. You and I get double messages from our leaders: "You must conserve energy." By this they do not mean resting your body, exercising your hard-earned right to laziness. They mean conserving natural gas, gasoline, crude oil, electricity. Yet at the same time, they say: "You must buy more homes that use natural gas; more cars that use more gasoline; more gadgets that use electricity. Furthermore, you must buy *new* cars, houses, gadgets, etc."

Creative laziness may at least call attention to these double messages. Creative laziness, if chosen as a way of life, may even turn the mad rush to the exhaustion of a "more and more," throw-away culture toward a more serene way of life. The more of these gadgets you buy, the more you have to get fixed and repaired when they break down. As I have said, few people want to do anything but to sell you a new one. The very art of learning to fix things for yourself can become a diversion from the eternal fog banks of the bureaucracies and the fatigue of status seeking. The sheer pleasure of sitting in a shoe shop while a comfortable and beloved pair of old shoes is being recycled into another year of wear is a permitted and earned form of doing nothing.

To do something about the "more and more" syndrome, then, you can use some of your native curiosity and leisure to figure out how some of your gadgets are made. You usually keep them without learning this. You prefer the mysteries of technology. All you want to know is what gadgets will do *for* you, not *how* they do it. If you already have the "thing," then a pleasant diversion would be to study *how* it works for you. Having learned this, you may discover many things about the gadget's upkeep and repair that you can do yourself. In fact, you will learn that maintenance is the better route than repair. If you cannot repair the "thing," then you can be more conversant with repair persons who can.

This leads to another pleasant avenue of diversion and using your right to laziness. *Tell the repair person you will wait for it!* Then he says or she says that there is no *way* you can wait. It will take two weeks before he or she can repair it. Then you can say, "Which day and at what time can I bring it back. I'll have to make two trips any how. I would do as well to bring it back and wait then!" Underneath this is a struggle of wills as to *who* is going to get the chance to be lazy, the repair person or you! It seems to me if shoe repair people will let you wait, if barbers *have* to have *you* there to do their work, the rest of the world can do so to some extent at least. You *rest* while they work for you! No one expects you to answer the phone while getting a haircut or a hairstyle. Then, too, you have the opportunity to find out *what* they did for you on the spot! You may even have the chance to learn *how* they fixed your gadget. If *you* have the same tools—or can buy the tools cheaper the next time—you might just fix it the next time yourself. All of these procedures are less trouble than calling twenty times to see if the "thing" is ready.

The main benefit of hanging around a repair shop, though, is that you can make friends with repair persons. The *interpersonal* enrichment of your relationship to your car, your lawn mower, your television, your radio, your vacuum cleaner as a *medium* between you and the persons who care for it *takes time.*

It takes some time in your town to *find* people who will cooperate with this admittedly eccentric way of doing things. I have one car repair shop all the way across my city where I can do this. I arrange a day ahead of time so they know I am coming. I take a book with me to read. I go to a nearby sandwich shop for lunch. After the crowd is scattered, the sandwich shop people like to just sit and converse while business is slack. No one knows me there by name, only by appearance. The telephone is not there. I can waste time and even read the fine print in my book. I can take a walk back and check in with how the job of repair is coming along. I find that the second set of brakes I have had installed on the old crate reveals to my very eyes that the wheel drums were not turned down and made "true" even when the first repair company did the job. I have paid these people for that work . . . 35,000 miles ago. They did not do it. Now, however, my repair friend who does not mind my direct inspection of his work and seems to do his work with a joyous pride, permits me to see what he is doing and what his predecessor did not do. He becomes my friend.

Later, too, when he has an illness and comes to our hospital, he has a friend in me who sees *our* "repair shop" from the inside. He knows he gets quality work. I like the feeling that he seems to be as proud of his work as our surgeons are of theirs. Yet, how frustrated he would be as a patient if his physicians had no time to explain to him somewhat leisurely what was wrong, what they were doing, and how they were doing it. It just may be that they are *not* in a hurry; they just have the habit of being in a hurry.

Such attitudes toward work and repair have built into the idea of work the importance of a certain deliberate casualness that allows, makes room for, and creates a kind of lazy way of working. Yet if we are hell bent upon overproduction, such reflectiveness does not happen. An example of this appeared recently in my community.

The Trappist Monastery at Gethsemani, Kentucky, the home of Thomas Merton in his latter years, is famous for its mild, semi-soft cheese. Their cheese is highly favored in distant places. It has often been a favored delicacy at the White

House. It is very much in demand. The Trappists are not at all eager about publicity for their cheese. "Publicity," one of the brothers says, "might bring in more orders for cheese." While he admits this might be hard to explain to a businessman, he says that the monks do not want any more orders. "We are not here to be cheese makers," he explained in a friendly manner. "We make cheese to make a living. Our life is a life of prayer. Cheese making is a routine we have to go through to support ourselves. Whether we are famous as cheesemakers does not faze us. Our main objective is God." (*Courier-Journal*, Louisville, Ky., March 3, 1977.) They know when to quit producing! The paradox of it all is that their cheese is, therefore, all the more in demand for the sheer reason of its scarcity and its high quality.

The workaholic has many diverse and distant psychological causes for his addiction to work in such a way as to make himself a slave. Each workaholic has his own particular set of dynamics pushing him past the point of exhaustion. However, all of us, confessed or unconfessed, workaholics are in the clutches of our desire for "it all." We "cotton" to wanting to produce more and more of whatever it is . . .

In our industrialized and commercialized world, Ivan Illich asks for the inversion of the tools of the world from the pure objective of productivity to that of "tools for convivial living." He expresses the hope for a world that "invert[s] the deep structure of tools . . . eliminating the need for either slave or masters and enhancing the person's range of freedom. People need . . . technology to make the most of the energy and imaginations one has rather than well-programmed energy slaves." (*Tools for Conviviality*, New York: Harper & Row, 1973, pp. 10–11.) Yet such broad-brush painting of the canvas of human life can best begin when honest workers like you, who have earned the right to leisure, begin to make laziness work in your behalf. You outwit being well-programmed energy slaves through the worship of the duties of overproduction, infinite expansion myths, and the derivation of your sense of personal worth from performance and productivity goals.

To Overcome Greed

We have spoken of the insatiable *need* of the work-addicted for "more and more." It would be well to strip the word "need" of its total misuse. You do not *need* 6,000 calories a day; you do not *need* a fifth of bourbon each morning and night. You do not *need* to work twenty-six hours a day, getting up two hours earlier each morning! You do not *need* all the overproduction of which we have been speaking. These are not *needs*. Overproduction is more often motivated by greed than need.

Greed is acquisitive desire beyond reason. This acquisitive desire takes central place in one's values. The classical biblical passage for this describes greed: "The love of money is the root of all evils; it is through this craving that some have wandered from the faith and pierced their hearts with many pangs." (I Timothy 6:10.) Behaviorally, greed may appear as refusal to engage in any pursuit except materially profitable work. You need to note this last sentence. The word "pursuit" appears in it. The inference is that the alternative life-style to greed is some other kind of *pursuit,* an aggressive activity. The thought of doing nothing, of loafing, of being at rest, of staring at the skies for an hour, of resting on a beach with the wind blowing sand upon one simply blows the greedy person's mind.

Among middle-aged persons of today, many greedy persons are those who either were born in poverty or met severe privation as adolescents and young adults during the Great Depression of the 1930s. They still live on the poverty ethic of always having a surplus. Now with that kind of programming, long after the immediate threat of starvation is past, we still revert to our ingrained insecurity. We had to lose face before others because of not having clothes to wear. We had to walk the streets without shelter looking for work that was not to be had. We are habituated to hold on to work compulsively long past necessity. The dynamic for this greed is the dynamic of some obesity: When urged to eat everything on one's plate and having been known to fight over and steal food, a person will tend to eat too much when in the presence of unlimited quantities of food.

Yet it is just such persons as this who have genuinely earned the right to laziness. *Letting go, taking some of the strain out of each day's life, taking a day to loaf, a week to rest, a month or even a year to retool one's energies in creative laziness may be the secret to the next fourth of one's life as surely as poverty and the Great Depression may be the secret to one's greed and overproduction now.* Creative laziness thus becomes an antidote for greed to be pursued as what William Glasser calls a "positive addiction." If massive amounts of hard work can offset poverty and hunger, then megavitamin doses of creative laziness ingeniously devised can offset the tyranny of greed and the "piercing of our hearts with many pangs" that the love of money and possessions has brought upon us.

You who read this book will ordinarily be a group of people who are nearly enough self-employed that you have some freedom to decide how much is enough. You do not *have* to be overproducers. You disguise your uncurbed hunger for more and more things, prestige, titles, certifications, etc. under such rationalizations as "laying aside for a rainy day," being sure that we are independent in our old age, and that *our* tenth of the working force works so that another tenth of the population may be on welfare, in retirement, etc. If you are partially educated in economics and thoroughly confused by economists, as I am, you may say, "When I work hard and make more money, and spend my money, it creates jobs for other people." This is the altruistic half-truth. If you worked discernibly less, then it would *allow* others to work more, also. Somewhere between the affluence of the work addict and the throttling back of overproduction to such an extent that unemployment takes over is a "Golden Mean." If followed with balance, you can permit yourself to live at the same time we are earning a living. How can you find this balance? Let me suggest some ways.

Sharing Work with Others

American society could say with Bertrand Russell: "We keep a large percentage of the working population idle, because we can dispense with their labor by making others overwork." (*In Praise of Idleness*, New York: Simon and Schuster, Inc., 1932, p. 21.) One must note that this was written in the time of the depths of the Great Depression in America . . . 1932. He says that in the past we had a "working class" and a "leisure class." The leisure class enjoyed advantages for which there was no basis in social justice; this necessarily made it oppressive, limited in its sympathies, and caused it to invent theories by which to justify its privileges. (Ibid., p. 26.) Russell goes further to suggest a four-hour work day. "In a world where no one is compelled to work more than four hours a day, every person possessed of scientific curiosity will be able to indulge it, and every painter will be able to paint without starving, however excellent his pictures may be. Young writers will not be obliged to draw attention to themselves by sensational pot boilers, with a view to acquiring the economic independence needed for monumental works, for which, when the time comes, they will have lost the taste and capacity . . . Medical men will have time to learn about the progress of medicine . . ." (Ibid., p. 28.)

Russell speaks of a Utopia when you look around you and see what the order of the day is. Can this happen on any large scale? By the time you and I got the bureaucratic machinery of government, business, and education to agree to the four-hour day, we would all be worked to a frazzle attending all the meetings of committees it would require. Maybe, though, you and I can make a few stabs in the right direction without asking anybody. The experience of a friend of mine may be helpful.

He discovered that after Wednesday afternoon, he was spending his whole time earning enough money to pay his taxes. The more he worked, the more he earned, the more he earned, the higher percentage the taxes took. He decided to figure out how much money was actually needed for the care of his family and his aging parents. Then he decided how much time and energy he would have to spend in order to meet those needs. When he was paying the Government one dollar out of every four he earned, he agreed in his own mind that to be a patriotic person he needed to work that much and pay that much taxes. Thus, when Thursday morning came he did not work any more that week. This did not work out too well. His fellow businessmen got out of touch with him. He decided to cut the length of his day instead of the week. Then he would work a decent six-hour day with a leisurely lunch and siesta time. The leisurely lunch and siesta became a positive addiction for him. He was there every day, but not all day.

What went with the rest of the work of my friend? He found a younger man (he himself was forty-two years old at the time). He began to share some of the clients with his younger colleague as he started his own business. He used the wisdom that I see evident in wiser physicians who become overtaxed. They find a person who is just beginning "to set up the practice" of medicine and start referring patients to them. They even take some of their funds and drop them back into medical education, enough money to make a young student's way financially possible.

The above case in point suggests that William Glasser, a psychiatrist, has developed a most noteworthy idea of "positive addiction." He rightly says that workaholism as I have defined it is based on the "sickness" model of alcohol addiction. When one works in psychiatric disaster clinics, as I do, this model is hard to miss and is not thereby nullified by Glasser's very accurate observation. However, if anything is to be done about workaholism, then a "positive addiction" must punctuate and change the whole life-style of the work addict. Therefore, I am heartily commending Glasser's six steps toward developing what he calls a "positive addiction." Running or jogging is an example he uses as well as various kinds of meditation.

Step One: Choose something non-competitive that you choose to do and can do for approximately one hour every day.

Step Two: Choose something you can do alone or with others but not something that depends upon others for you to do it.

Step Three: Choose something that you do easily and that does not take a great deal of mental effort to do it well.

Step Four: Believe that if you persist at it you will improve your whole outlook on life because it has a real, enjoyable value—spiritual, physical, or mental—for you.

Step Five: Choose something that you do not have to consult someone else as to whether it is improving you. You be the judge.

Step Six: Choose something that you can do without being critical of yourself because if you cannot accept yourself during the time of the activity, it will not be addicting. (*Positive Addiction,* New York: Harper & Row, 1976, p. 92ff.)

While you are enjoying your "positive addiction" you can make friends by sharing surplus work with others. Whatever the position you may hold, when you follow the practice of sharing some of your work with others, you will find that both frustration and satisfaction attends the process. If at all possible, it is important that they do this work in their *own name,* not yours. If you allow yourself to be personally responsible for their actions, then you are in more trouble than you started with. You are likely to retreat from sharing. You may say, "If you want a thing done right, do it yourself." The question is: "Do you want to get into the system of teaching protégés?" Developing protégés is similar to but greatly different from simply sharing your work with others.

Developing Protégés

A protégé is a person who is under the care and protection of another. He or she is covered or shielded from that which would injure, destroy, or detrimentally affect him or her. One who chooses a protégé commits himself to secure or protect that person against attack, encroachment, harm, and disintegration insofar as it is needed. The world of work as we know it often reminds one of a jungle; at other times one gets images of swimming in shark-infested waters. The person who has learned the arts of survival in the world of work has some need of an ethic of work that includes teaching those arts of survival to younger, less-experienced persons. Most of the people who have really earned the right to laziness have ceased to need to be insecure about their own survival in the work force, except at their most vulnerable point: They themselves are likely to destroy themselves by leaving their own right to laziness unactivated. All around them, then, they will find younger and less-experienced persons who are dazzled by their accomplishments. These younger colleagues worry about the health and safety of their seniors because of their overwork and lack of care of themselves. From this population of persons younger than yourself can come your own protégés who genuinely have your well-being at heart. These protégés would really like to learn the trade secrets of the older maestro, ballerina, salesperson, or whatever masculine-feminine equation of the thought of a hardworking and successful professional, artisan, artist, etc., you would choose to use.

Basic issues are hidden in developing protégés in order to set oneself free for some honestly earned leisure. Let's uncover them.

Control is the first one. You do not turn loose of your work and let go and rest while others share it as your protégés because you are power-hungry and want to control events past, present, and future. You lose that control when you turn some of your work over to a protégé.

Trust is the second issue. Consciously you may say that you cannot trust the person's lack of experience. More profoundly you may be really saying that you cannot trust the person to look after our best interests as well as your own. These younger persons may be likened unto birds learning to fly. Some of them, however, may be likened unto robins or some other bird you would choose as a very specially loved and

cared-for bird. Others may be likened unto birds of a scav-
enger order—such as the vulture. You love and trust the one,
you loathe and distrust the other. The work addict is likely to
assume that all birds are of one kind or another, to be loved
and trusted completely or to be looked upon as vultures out to
get him.

In the first instance, the work addict becomes a roosting
tree for all sorts of extractive, dependent, and/or recklessly
ambitious persons. In the second instance, the work addict becomes the suspicious, self-appointed user of people as accou-
terments of his vanity. Thus, people age unnecessarily. However, a goal of maturity is to have your love and affection for
persons seasoned through experience and empowered with
discernment. Can you discern the difference between robins
and vultures? If so, you have a gift of the human spirit to be
treasured and sought after with inner discipline and meditation. Once you are able to "let go" of the need to control everything and to discern whom to trust and whom to allow to
be the vultures without adding yourself to their diet, then the
experience of developing protégés becomes a senior-junior
sharing of tasks happily and with serenity.

The third issue is the ability to come down off one's high
horse and comfortably be a *colleague* with a protégé. The
ideal protégé relationship is one into whose hands portions of
work may be placed without any strings attached that require
the overworked person to supervise. The protégé is a younger
peer. In fact, the protégé *could* manage the whole operation
trustworthily while the chief is away. This would allow some
lazy time for the chief.

Such hopes and plans have the makings of a bureaucracy.
One faces the dilemma of getting some release from work for
the exercise of the right of laziness, on the one hand, and the
hazards of developing a hierarchical structure that takes more
work to manage, on the other hand. This dilemma has been
variously approached by the use of Parkinson's Law, the Peter
Principle, and Petrie's Law.

The popular statement of Parkinson's Law is one way of
explaining why bureaucracies burgeon. Parkinson's Law says

that bureaucratic staffs increase in inverse proportion to the amount of work done. When a manager appoints ten people to help him to get the work done, then an eleventh one has to be appointed to see to it that these ten do their work. These, in turn, become supervisors and increase in number themselves until directors have to be appointed over them to see to it that they do their work. The process goes on *ad infinitum*. The person at the top of the pyramid loses all contact with and control over what is going on in the infrastructures. His own efforts become counterproductive. The underlying assumption is that no one is going to do his work. Someone else should be made responsible for seeing to it that he is not lazy. "Empire builders" usually go this route. The assumption that the worker is a vulture who "eats up the profits and production" by not working ferments distrust. The stress of the unhappiness uses more energy than the work itself would if done by reasonably unfatigued workers who are trusted to do their job well because they are considered and been proven to be competent.

Lawrence J. Peter has stated a second hazard of appointing persons to do your work for you. This is the hazard of promoting a protégé to levels in the hierarchy that are beyond his competence. The assumption is that if one is a laborer who does his work well, he will make a good supervisor over the last ten persons to be appointed. If he is a good supervisor, then he will make an ideal director. Then the person has been promoted—usually very rapidly without any real evidence of competence in the previous positions. He is beyond the kind of work for which he was trained. Probably he would do something else most happily if it were not for insatiable needs to have more status and perquisites of position—plush offices, private toilets, echelons of secretaries, expense accounts, and memberships in the local prestige clubs. The advantage of this kind of person to the chief executive is that he is weak enough and incompetent enough to be merely an extension of the executive's own ego needs and not an autonomous worker in one's own right. He does only what the executive wishes. The executive is usually too absorbed in his own pursuits to convey what those wishes are. The result is that a person who was previously competent at a task from which he was removed in order to assist the executive now becomes little more than a highly paid maid or valet for the executive. (Laurence J. Peter and Raymond Hull, *The Peter Principle*, New York: William Morrow, 1969.)

Petrie's Law is the third hard-earned lesson from developing protégés. Petrie's Law is based on a "fewer the better" view of getting work done. Jesus of Nazareth is cited as one who selected protégés. He showed us that when you have more than eleven persons, even twelve, you have one too many! Petrie's Law is based on the revolutionary concept of competence and compensation. The objective is to get a few of the most competent persons to be found. Pay them equal salaries of a large size. Expect them to get the job done themselves. If they need anyone to help them, they are to employ that person out of their own funds. Thus, they discover that they do not need nearly as many people—poorly paid—to get the job done as they at first thought they would need. This "repeals" Parkinson's Law.

Robert Townsend tells of having been made an executive in American Express. If they were to make it at all, they would have to give up secretaries, assistants, supervisors, and directors. He discovered that having no subordinates, the personnel wrote briefer reports, had fewer memoranda, depended more on face-to-face conversation with persons. They saved time by throwing out 90 per cent of the junk they had been filing. As the executive, he says, "The transition was accomplished gradually and without an overall increase in the budget. What the 21-person pyramid evolved into was a 13-person partnership of peers. My job as senior partner was to get us the tools we needed and keep the rest of the company off our backs." (*Horizon*, Winter, 1973. Published in *Intellectual Digest*, August 1973, Vol. III, No. 12, p. 56.)

This approach Townsend contrasts with what he calls the Motor Vehicle Bureau Syndrome: "Start, say, with 10,000 employees. Put them all into one building and divide them into departments. When the communication breaks down, develop inter- and intra-office memo forms and a policy manual. When expenses begin to get out of hand, develop rigid salary limits and layers of salary committees. Develop purchasing forms and procedures so that it takes six months to get a desk lamp. When the best people get frustrated and leave, each will be replaced by a warm body. Soon you'll have 16,000 sullen timeservers, each bitterly resentful of customer intrusions and bent on getting even with the company." (Ibid., p. 57.)

Three approaches—the Parkinson Law, the Peter Principle and Petrie's Law. All three have one thing in common: They are strategies for dealing with laziness in the organization, a topic we will deal with more explicitly in the next chapter. Another way of putting it is that there are ways of getting people motivated to work, i.e., out of their lassitude, laziness, and indolence. The appeal of the Parkinson Law is that of proving oneself able to get to supervise others. The appeal of the Peter Principle is that of status without competence or responsibility to function. The appeal of the Petrie's Law is competency and intimacy in a peer group of persons who respect and trust each other and want to get the job done with the least hassle.

Young persons who have heard me discuss the right to laziness tend to be discouraged by the prospects of being able to earn the right to laziness. They are heavily involved in capturing the right to work, the opportunity to demonstrate their competence, the chance to earn a living. They build habits of working long hours at slavelike and often meaningless tasks, simply because they do not have seniority and position. They are underpaid for their work. Only occasionally do they have a middle-aged person like you to develop a peership with them by reviewing at least the perils of seniority and privilege, i.e., the peril of wanting to control all who work around him or her; the peril of empire building; the peril of trusting no one but one's palace guard absolutely; the peril of working longer and longer days with no permission from one's self or situation to break out of the slavery and exercise the earned right to laziness; the peril of becoming so over-identified with your work or your institution that you have no real existence

apart from it; the peril of work-addiction with no positive re-
placement for its negative destructiveness.

My own personal encounter with these perils prompts me to
invite a collaborative senior-partner/junior-partner relationship with young persons. Elderly persons who are already
retired out of the competitive rat race are often exceptionally
adept at this skill. I watch them and learn from them. Doing
so has pushed me to deeper levels of appreciation of the right
to plan one's own schedule, the right to invest one's time in
places where it is most meaningful and useful, and the opportunity to reflect on the meaning of the lives of those who are
younger in relation to my own life's meaning. The liaison with
these younger persons is distinctly that of investment of life in
protégés. Yet it calls for an articulate description of my own
place and role in human affairs. Let me call this "living the
peripheral way of life," "living on the boundary" of things.
The peripheral or boundary existence is my own way of maintaining and exercising my right to laziness. I will have jolly
well earned this right with a forty-seven-year work record,
with five years more to go before I will be sixty-five, the time
when institutions retire personnel. Retirement, though, is re-
pugnant to me; it means to me that I will change my arena of
work to fit my health.

Living on the Periphery

Making laziness work for us calls for a creative and consciously chosen life-style. I am suggesting the way of life of
living on the periphery or at the boundaries of life. I was introduced to this idea by a young colleague of mine named
Thomas Chapman. He and his wife, Brenda, are two of the
very few young people I know who have deliberately chosen
to live a life on the periphery of the fixed roles of the occupa-
tional world. They have moved to a small Midwestern city
and have developed a protégé relationship to a retired farmer
and his wife. Together they are seeking to develop a wild life

preserve, a retreat center, and a place where stress-ridden persons can interrupt their stress and not be faced with another harried schedule. They have chosen to call their project "Eurisko," meaning to search, to seek.

Tom Chapman introduced me to a very important quotation from Aldous Huxley's book, *Ape and Essence* (New York: Harper & Brothers, 1948, pp. 6–10). I quote it in its entirety: "It is not at the center, not from within the organization, that the saint can cure our regimented insanity; it is only from without, at the periphery. If he makes himself a part of the machine, in which the collective madness is incarnated, one or the other of two things is bound to happen. Either he remains himself, in which case the machine will use him as long as it can and, when he becomes unusable, reject or destroy him. Or, he will be transformed into the likeness of the mechanism with and against which he works, and in this case we shall see Holy Inquisitions and alliances with any tyrant prepared to guarantee ecclesiastical privileges." "The machine" is the organization, the prestige system, the power structure, whether it be a business, a school, a church denomination, a political order, or a family heritage. Studies of stress indicate that the "thing" from which you and I need to be delivered is the kinds of intense hassles that occur in a status system the closer to the center of it we get. These are the kinds of "work" that demand the most of you. At the same time they enchant you with fictitious images of your "glorified self" in all their power. These are the kinds of "work" that turn what would be a healthy seven- or eight-hour day into a disastrous twelve- and fifteen-hour day of work. The difference is made up of "mouth wrestling" meetings that produce little or no satisfaction. Such meetings send you home to sleepless indecision as to whether to stay in or get out of the hassles. Yet the thing that keeps you at the center of things is the deadly pride of the position. To affect these processes from the outside rather than from the center, from the periphery, as it were, gives you a power of choice. You can take the option of a serene kind of unambitiousness that may be called laziness. If so, you can identify with those who call it laziness.

They weigh the worth of a person by the *place* he or she is in the organization and not by the *person* who he or she really is and the competence which he or she functions in relation to other persons.

This does not mean that you or I are uninvolved. It means simply that we are involved differently. More influence can be exerted by a free John the Baptist in the desert than a power-imprisoned Herod who has to get directions from others to do the wrong thing. This stance toward life can be taken by a young person who insists on competence and independence and does not become politically obligated, sold out, or ingratiated to by too many beguiling gifts from people who would "use" him or her. A considerable number of young persons out of the counterculture of the sixties, like Thomas Chapman, can live simply enough and close enough to the necessities of life to maintain their freedom as a person. A few persons who are in their middle-age years maintain a *diversity* of ways of earning a living. They are sufficiently nonchalant about getting both prestigious offices and the perquisites of such offices that their lives have remained at base simple and free of a lot of trappings. They can live on the periphery by the "weight of their being" as persons and not by reason of the particular "connections," "platforms," or "positions" they have. They have not permitted themselves to become "entangled" in what Aldous Huxley calls "guaranteed" hierarchical privileges. The human spirit was created for this kind of freedom. The purpose of redemption is to restore that kind of freedom if it has been lost. Free persons were never meant to be slaves. Free persons live at the periphery of slave systems. Moses lived at the periphery of the tyranny of both the prior bad decisions of his Hebrew forefathers and the tyranny of the blandishments of the royalty of Egypt.

In this sense the right to rest, renewal, contemplation, meditation, and doing nothing becomes an aspect of the freedom of the human spirit. When I suggest to a distraught businessman, physician, minister, or housewife that the massive stress they are suffering must be interrupted by two to three days of simple rest at a nearby state park, they regularly say that they

are not free to do so. Yet, if they did not feel themselves to be
at the very center of everything and could feel "peripherality,"
then they could stand the change. They could make their own
laziness work for them. The freedom to make a simple two-
day decision *can* be an option for the "peripheral person."
What is such a person like?

1. The peripheral person does not expect a "kingdom of his
or her own" that will outlast him or her. Such persons who do
expect this of themselves and their world are often referred to
as "king makers." They want to control, not only the days of
their own years, but the shape of all succeeding generations.
The peripheral person is one who has learned the hard way
that "king makers" are in reality "pearl casters." They cast
their pearls of influence in the direction of the persons whom
they "tap" to be their successors. This is a weird, time-bound
attempt to reincarnate themselves before their own eyes. To
do this to another person is to treat that person whom they
appoint as an animal. Jesus chose the animal "swine" as a
symbol. Casting pearls before persons who are both treated
and see themselves as little more than swine causes them to
turn and rend the pearl caster. This is the plight of the pearl
caster. The peripheral person has either never taken up or has
renounced the "king maker" syndrome. One of the most pa-
thetic examples of the king-making process is the Eisenhower-
Nixon effort. After the 1961 defeat of Richard Nixon as a candidate for presidency, Dwight Eisenhower was asked what
was the greatest disappointment of his presidency and the
years that immediately followed. He said that the loss of the
election by Nixon was his greatest disappointment.

2. The peripheral person has consciously chosen to deepen
his or her life perceptions and relationships rather than to ex-
pand to the point of being spread too thin. The peripheral
person has from the outset been the kind of person who
chooses depth over superficiality, face-to-face relationships
over impersonal ones, and refuses to say yes to every demand.
Instead of perceiving himself as a sophisticated Occidental
computer who keeps *all* in mind, the peripheral person lets
the computers be the computers and insists on being a finite,

forgetful, sometimes-remembering person who needs all the help available in keeping things in focus. Instead of being an all-seeing eye, the all-hearing ear, he lets others do their share and remains open and teachable as to what they have seen and heard.

3. Given his preference, the peripheral person would rather be a consultant than a member of the power structure of the staff of any given organization. He would prefer to be peripherally related to many different systems of human life than absorbed at the center of any one system. When it comes to power, he would rather have a weight of being and a power of presence than a bureaucratic office. Bernard Baruch exemplified this in his day. He said that he had only a park-bench interest in administration. Yet even Presidents of the country sought his wisdom. You do not have to be rich in money to do this; you do have to be free of the need to supervise the whole system of things. Even the administrator at the core of things could come to terms with the reality that just being the central administrator puts him at the periphery of what causes the organization to work. Patients cause a hospital to work. Students cause a school to work. Customers cause a business to work. The administrator facilitates the care of patients, the teaching of students, and the servicing of customers. The difference between effective administrators and ineffective ones is directly related to their awareness of people, patients, students, customers, etc. who actually make the thing work or not work.

4. The peripheral person knows how to vacate. To vacate is a form of the noun "vacation." Literally, it means to empty. The peripheral person has this attitude of "emptying" himself or herself of the trappings and perquisites of position. These are not things that pre-occupy him. He does not grasp after them or mistake them for his own. In the New Testament, this emptying is called "kenosis" in the Apostle Paul's description of Jesus of Nazareth. He lived at the periphery of all the power structures of Judaism. He died outside the gates of Jerusalem. Yet he was and is a more functional person than all leaders.

Harry Truman made a clear distinction between his person and the office he held as President of the United States. He said that the President who assumed that the 21-gun salute was *for him,* that the "Hail to the Chief" was *for him* was in trouble. He said: "That is for the Presidency, not for the man who happens to be in office at a brief span of time." This is vacating. The person who has this mind of "vacating," can leave the job, the crowd, the success, the acquisition of power and things in order to rest, to re-create, to meditate, to pray, to think, to reflect, to loaf, to do nothing in the process of being genuinely human.

CHAPTER 3

Vacating, Free Time, and Vacations

S t. Augustine said in his *Confessions:* "*Si nemo ex me quaeret, scio; si quaerenti explicare velim, nescio.*" Translated, this means: "If no one asks me, I know; if I wish to explain to one who asks, I know not." (Book XI, Chap. XIV.) When one asks what free time, leisure, or the opportunity to do nothing is, it is difficult if not impossible to explain. Before the question is asked, everyone would assume that he or she knows. I have already given one explanation of vacation or free time as the opportunity "to vacate," turning the noun into a verb. This means to leave, to leave empty, to change places, or just plain "get out of here." Some clues to the nature of the laziness we are to make work for us begin to emerge from what is hidden in the mystery of familiarity, i.e., the meaning of vacating, free time, and/or a vacation.

What Is a Vacation?

Sebastian deGrazia says that perhaps we can "judge the inner health of a land by the capacity of its people to do nothing—to lie abed, to amble about aimlessly, to sit having a coffee—because whoever can do nothing, letting his thoughts go where they may, must be at peace with himself." (*Of*

Time, Work and Leisure, New York: The Twentieth Century Fund, 1962 p. 341.) Yet men such as Arnold Toynbee, a confessed work addict, say that the reason people cannot vacate, do nothing, enjoy a vacation, etc. is that we are afraid of our own solitude. The Chinese philosopher Lin Yutang says that the true purpose of travel "should be to become lost and unknown." He chides vacationers who bring along with them handsful of letters of introduction so that they will become known wherever they are. Anonymity is better; to have no fixed hours, no mail, no inquisitive neighbors. "A man stands a poorer chance of discovering himself as a human being if he brings along with him letters of introduction, and of finding out exactly how God made him if he brings along with him letters of introduction, and of finding out exactly how God made him as a human being, apart from the artificial accidents of social standing." (*The Importance of Living,* New York: John Day, 1937, p. 331.)

From this point of vantage, the meaning of laziness put to work for us and of a vacation, then, means *emptying ourselves of our multiple roles in life.* This is a very difficult thing to do. I recall a venture of mine into using an afternoon of my days off to go to a health spa. One Saturday I was moving from the steam room to the sauna. I got seated in the sauna room when a young man came into the room and also sat down. He said "hello" to me and I mumbled some kind of greeting back. We sat there a while in silence. He then spoke to me and said, "Aren't you a professor?" I said, "Yes." He said, "Thought so. I can tell these things!" There I sat in shorts in a sauna and I was pegged as a professor! Yet, with only a pair of bathing trunks on I took my role with me. To the contrary, I feel as I did when I drove into a hospital parking lot to visit a patient. We parked near a parking zone for "Doctors Only" "Clergy Only." I mused to myself, "I don't mind being a professor. In fact, I enjoy it. But being a professor *only,* I absolutely refuse to be!" I insist on basic selfhood as a human being before all the "roles" of life, but saying so is easier than causing it to happen. What would it be like to be a "Professor Only"? No wonder so many professors are dull!

This is what Lin Yutang means by a vacation, i.e., to rediscover one's basic humanness apart from the accustomed roles of life. The person who cannot thus be a stranger to others will remain a stranger to himself or herself. The reluctance to get to know oneself hurries us back to work where our roles insulate us from the terror of meeting ourselves as we really are. The prestige roles we are accustomed to wearing are like medieval armor as we clank from one duty on the job to another. No wonder we are so tired that we do not know why.

The Laziness Gauge of Time

When we probe further into the meaning of "to vacate, to have free time, to take a vacation, to making laziness work for us," we get fuzzier and fuzzier in our own minds as to what this kind of time is. Total rest provides a gauge for clarifying the use of time. DeGrazia divides time into four kinds: *Work and work-related time; subsistence time,* or time that we use in sleeping, eating, cooking, shopping, maintaining a place to sleep, going to the bathroom and repairing the body, and extensions of the body such as cars, home appliances, etc.; *free time,* as opposed to time spent in work or in subsistence; and *all the rest,* denoting time spent in making love, attending church, etc. He concludes on mathematical guess that the average amount of free time a person has in our industrialized communities and business communities is about 2½ hours a day. He makes note that this implies a six-day work week, inasmuch as most workers seem to have more need for money than free time and add to the official five-day work week a sixth one of double-jobbing in the evenings and/or Saturdays. From casual observation one can observe some farmers, business persons, and blue collar persons spend seven days a week at some sort of remunerative work.

The core of the problem seems to be that a preponderance of persons prefer to make more money to having more free time. If the person is not making more money, he is *saving* more money by do-it-yourself improvements of the capital outlay of their homes and/or cars, or simply standing in line four hours to buy a new piece of furniture for half price. Time spent in accurate record keeping for income tax purposes, for keeping insurance companies accountable for what is owed on health bills, etc. can be considered making money by saving money. The Utopian ideal of the four-hour work day overlooks the hard reality of people preferring more money to more free time. Tangled up in this web of motives is the sense of self-worth that is weighed and measured by the amount of money that one can heap up in a given length of time. The trouble is that the *given length of time* is not mentioned along with the money. The person who says he earns $10,000 a year, or $100,000 a year may really be a $5,000 or a $50,000 a year person who works two shifts. Self-employed persons can learn very, very much from studying the attitudes of hourly shift workers. These persons talk about time and a half for overtime and double time for work on weekends and holidays. The self-employed professional would do well to consider this in his calculation of the worth of a work week. If you and I do not value our time, no one else will likely do so. If we are going to build an idea of our self-worth on the amount of income we earn, then we need to be consciously careful about the worth of our work time.

Whereas deGrazia's four-fold classification of time is very helpful when seen from the standpoint of the impingement of work upon free time, it does not assess the amount of stress involved in different types of time use. When we assess the use of time in terms of the stress involved, we get a different kind of classification. I would suggest four uses of time from the vantage point of stress:

1. Coping with hindrances to satisfactory discharge of one's duties, such as trying to get the company to furnish a typewriter for a typist, or untangling a computer foul-up on the pay of one's associate, or simply trying to get into one's office during six weeks of delayed construction, etc.

2. Joyful work in fulfilling one's sense of purpose in life and satisfying results for his efforts. Many people look on this kind

of work as a sort of "play" that can be done effortlessly. By this they mean that the stress factor in work is next to zero in this kind of work. It is a different kind of work time qualitatively.

3. Diversionary activities that change the pace, change the place, change the nature of the activity, change the degree of enjoyment, relieve the amount of stress. Shifts from mental work to physical work and/or vice versa also help. An example of this would be working on a car after having been composing a manuscript on a typewriter as I am doing now. Sports and physically active recreation take this turn, too.

4. Rest and reflection uses of time in sleep, meditation, staring, breathing deeply with full concentration upon breathing, sitting inert in a tub of warm water, dozing in a chair, goofing off, make laziness work for us. In my estimate, a vacation consists of either diversions from work or of rest and reflection. To vacate means to free up time for diversionary activities or straight rest, or both. The use of the laziness gauge of time in terms of removing stress and reducing strain through diversion and rest enables a person to make clean decisions about making laziness work for him or her.

Stress Wisdom and Vacations

We have learned much about stress and stress management in the meticulous studies of persons like Hans Selye, Roy Grinker and John Spiegel, and Peter Bourne. This wisdom enables us to make laziness work for us and assures maximum good judgment in planning diversions and rest periods. Some of the maxims about stress management are as follow:

1. A definite end to a particular piece of work, combat, or aggravation makes the stress more bearable. Therefore, a rhythm of "endings" and end-points in time make the effort less stressful. In World War II, we were all in the war "for the duration," and the end of the war was not predictable. In Vietnam, the "short-timer" was there for a year or thirteen months

at most. He knew *when* his part of the war would be over. This end made the effort more tolerable. On a job, to plan blocks of work with specific finishing points is a wise way to schedule "breathers," slack time, goof-off time. Deadlines have a creative use in planning *when* to be lazy. If a vacation is set well ahead of time, then anticipation becomes a better part of delight.

2. Intermittent interruptions of work are a form of stress reduction. For our staff, who are accustomed to half-hour lunch breaks, to take an hour or an hour and a half as a group and go to a place outside the Medical Center for lunch is a real diversion. In the countries that have ritualized the siesta, total rest is a sequel to lunch. The evening meal is later than that of Americans, and people lounge around the table in various stages of consciousness. In speaking of "vacations on the job" I will speak more of these interruptions.

3. Responding to pain intelligently. A dry throat and mouth, a distended bladder and/or bowel communicate discomfort and some pain. After much stress pain will localize in the more vulnerable parts of the body. After exorbitant amounts of stress, pain will generalize and the person hurts all over worse than he does anywhere else. The immediate relief of the body's needs for hydration, urination, and defecation is a civil right to that rare bit of solitude in the john to which everyone is entitled to respond on demand! Persistent pain in one place will tend to be relaxed through diversions. If not, diagnosis by a physician is indicated. Generalized pain in every bone and muscle indicates total rest, a break with the reality known as work.

4. Reducing the number of sensory inputs of decisions to be made. Stress can be lowered by a salesperson by reducing the number of clients sought each day. A physician can reduce his or her stress by deciding how many patients can be seen on a planned basis each day, allowing plenty of time for interruption by telephone and acute emergencies. We are back again to whether "more and more" is the answer to a better quality of work and serenity of being.

5. Deciding on the length of the day and week. The self-

employed person has certain latitude in deciding on the length of his day. The blue collar worker can decide how much double jobbing is really necessary. A poorly paid professor can decide on how many outside engagements will be used to supplement income, etc. This regulates the length of the day and week.

We can determine what a vacation is on the stress profile just given by taking sleep as the paradigm or working example of a daily vacation. Sleep is as symbolic of the kind of laziness required in waking hours to introduce vacating as a way of life and not just as a time of the year when we travel long miles, spend much money, stand in long lines, have wrecks, and feel guilty about not working. This paradigm of sleep, however, does not elude the commercialism of modern tourism. How often have you had trouble sleeping in a fancy motel or hotel and begun calculating how much money you were wasting by not sleeping when just to have a bed to lie upon has cost you approximately $3.00 per hour, conservatively speaking? Sleep, nevertheless, gathers up the raveling sleeve of care and provides us with that total withdrawal for external stimuli and the meeting of our internal stimuli in dreams, half-sleeping "great ideas," and eludes the worst of work's tenacious grip upon us.

Vacating as a Daily Way of Life

If we called sleep 10 on a scale of ten defining respite from work, we could work out 9 other gradations for vacating as a daily activity known as "doing nothing."

10=Sleep
 9=Personal and private prayer/meditation
 8=Reverie and absent-minded staring
 7=Solitude away from abundance of stimuli
 6=Anonymity at whatever place
 5=Paid vacation with no connection to work
 4=Self-chosen vacation with no connection to work

3=Vacation to catch up on personally chosen and not imposed chores

2=Diversions on the job

1=Joyful work

0=Hassling the system on the job and being hassled by the system on the job

A similar negative scale could be worked out to indicate how work gradually turns into slavery:

—1=Cleaning up after the incompetence of others: *Fatigue*

—2=Taking over duties left by a reduction in personnel or created by the increase of the production and programs: "the stretch-out system." *Anger at injustice*

—3=Being denied the necessary tools and materials with which to work. *Helplessness*

—4=Working at a task one would not choose if it were not for the salary and benefits that this job provides. *Trappedness*

—5=Being expected and required to work both day and night and on weekends without compensatory time off or increase in pay. *Being Used*

—6=Being used by one employer(s) to do things that are at best beneath one's level of competence and one's sense of dignity or at worst are either unethical or illegal or both. *Humiliation*

—7=Being stripped of opportunity for advancement and growth but yet being expected to accept responsibilities without adequate authority to discharge them. *Hopelessness*

—8=Being harassed by one's employer(s) with the deliberate objective of causing one to resign. *Passive Aggressiveness*

—9=Being indentured to the corporation or institution by loans, external expectations of one's family to the point one cannot resign and change jobs. *Indentured Service*

—10=Being committed to resign but unable to get another job. *Slavery*

If you will locate yourself on these positive and negative scales, you will have your own "vacating ability" index. The quantum known as "joyful work" is the criterion for which we strive in work-as-play happiness and creativity. The negative factors from —1 to —10 are those that make of work a thing to escape, whether on the job or off the job. These negative factors lead to the "insincere uses of laziness" to be discussed in the next chapter. They are indicators for a change of job, without which either the gamesmanship of insincere laziness or the illnesses associated with laziness as a symptom appear as described in Chapter 5.

The gradual transmutation of work into slavery from an experience of joy is not a new idea. I was pleasantly surprised to discover a treatise by Leo Tolstoy written in 1900. (*The Slavery of Our Times*, New York: Dodd, Mead & Co., 1900, p. 88.) He pointed out that the lack of land and the weight of taxes drive people to compulsory work. All the while their own increased desires and appetites and unsatisfied needs decoy persons into slavery kinds of work and keep them at it. Yet it is just this kind of slavery from which the discipline of our desires and needs and the recognition of the need for freedom and the right to make laziness work for us can with wisdom deliver us. The freedom to get away from this kind of slavery, the opportunity to do exactly what you want to do, and to choose not to do anything is what a young second-year college student defines as a vacation. My conclusion is that a vacation can happen either on or off the job, depending on whether the work is a joyful work or a kind of slavery. Ordinarily, however, a vacation is either the use of a diversion or straight rest to interrupt the stress of any kind of work situation.

Vacations on the Job

Joyful work has built into it what Milton Berle is quoted as calling "instant vacations." Let me suggest a few illustrations of these instant vacations on the job.

1. *The entry of a child into the work area.* For whatever reason, children do come into a broad spectrum of work areas. They tend to introduce the element of diversion, play, and respite from work. A plane is loading its passengers. Most of these passengers are business persons for whom the trip is a job. A young mother enters with a baby in one arm and leading an older child who can walk. She has all of the baby gear with her, a little like supplies for a small army. Instantly first one and then the other businessman vies with his fellow passengers to turn the care of the child into an easier task for the mother and a diversion for the men on business missions. Just what I can do with this illustration for the pediatrician whose whole day is spent with children entering the work area is hard to say. I assume that this is one of those situations where a helping adult entering the work area produces an instant vacation.

2. *The use of humor.* The pleasant interlude of a good story well told produces laughter, another instant vacation of the job. What bedraggled student listening to tedious detail in a lecture does not breathe more deeply, lean back and stretch, and laugh when the lecturer or fellow student introduces genuine humor into the classroom work! Spontaneous humor generated by the situation itself is better than rehearsed stories. The student who raises his hand and asks to ask a question and then, being given permission, asks the class if everyone is as bored as he is strikes me as a very funny situation, even if I am the person giving the lecture. Simply to admit that boredom arises out of a sense of helplessness with a given set of problems and that I feel the helplessness to make the stuff come alive myself is a breath of fresh air in a class on statistics or any of a long list I can remember.

3. *The sudden appearance of the regal and majestic in the line of duty.* Like the Galilean, Jesus of Nazareth, majesty does not always appear in pomp and circumstance. It appears unexpectedly to "make a day" for toiling persons. For example, I was working with Mrs. Owens, a black nurse, in the care of patients. We came to an interruption and she remarked that I was wearing a cardigan sweater like Jimmy

Carter. I told her even though both he and I are Southerners, Southern Baptists, and wear cardigan sweaters, there was a major difference: he is President of the United States and I am not. Then I commented that it is interesting how the peanut and the soybean have been the purveyors of hope to people. George Washington Carver discovered both freedom and economic hope for himself and his people in his study of the peanut. People in the deep South had diversified their crops from cotton to peanuts and soybeans and found liberation from slavery to cotton. Now we have a Southern peanut farmer who has been elected President with the hope that this really means that the Civil War is over.

In response to this, Mrs. Owens told me a story about her mother. She said that her mother had her first child at the age of thirteen. She had only a third-grade education. However, as each child started school, her mother would insist that the child teach her what he or she had learned in school. In this way she became educated by her own children. Mrs. Owens said, "My mother was a childlike person. She could learn from her own children." I sensed an entry of the majestic in her description of her mother. Mrs. Owens demonstrates that same regal quality. We had experienced an interlude in the midst of work as if we had been to another continent in a moment's time.

4. *The drama of personal intimacy and caring.* The day's work is occasionally punctuated by a quiet drama of intimacy and caring. I recall the depths of such a drama I felt come my way in the work of the chief engineer at Naval Ordnance. Our older son works there. He is a technical assistant of the chief engineer. At this time, our son was on a highly dangerous mission in Vietnam in 1972. He was wounded in the line of his duties. I received a telephone call from the chief engineer telling about the shrapnel wound our son had received in his leg. A day or so later he brought to our home the exact wording of the communique in print. Each time he talked to my son by radio telephone in Vietnam, he would relay messages back and forth between us. This man and I formed a comradeship that is deep and wonderful, filled with care and closeness of

friendship. In his day's work as a chief engineer in a weaponry division of the Navy and my work as a teacher, it is a breather, a respite, a "get-away" sort of vacation within the job when he and I meet for lunch, share common concerns, and get acquainted with each other's world. Now that my son is back home, safe and well, all three of us share a closeness of care for each other.

5. *Avoidance of interpersonal "tailgating" in a bumper-to-bumper existence.* I read about six investigative reporters who took to the highways to see what is really happening to the national 55-mile speed limit. Great numbers of motorists passed them. Only rarely did they pass anyone else. The most hazardous thing that happened to them was when a person behind them, often a large truck, would get bumper to bumper with them tailgating them at 55 miles per hour. They would become somewhat terror-stricken until they could get into the right lane and let the truck pass. Sticking to the bumper-to-bumper routine, whether the "bumper" or the "bumpee," is a way of making any kind of relationship both taxing and hazardous.

The reporters' experience is a parable for living the day's work with broad, safe spaces between relationship-responsibilities. The salesperson who plans calls on prospective customers too closely together hazards losing both customers. The contractor who contracts completion dates on houses or commercial buildings lives in a pressure-cooker if he programs completion and beginning dates too closely. The physician who plans more appointments than any one afternoon can contain may make more enemies than he gets people well. The counselor who has clients one after another with no breaks in between is running a bumper-to-bumper course. These persons have little or no time to reflect upon their own work, to savor the uniqueness of each human relationship, to sense the vistas from side to side without looking at the "next" transaction ahead.

To plan life on the job, inasmuch as possible, with times between for "breathers," "pit stops," looking around, catching a moment of reverie, going to the john, for giving thanks, for a bit of celebration, for a call home to one's lover (or to his or her work)—to plan life on the job this way is to build minute vacations into the job itself. But most of us have taxi meters for brains, ticking away, translating space and time into money. Such brains do not know the things we are talking about here. Such brains *can* be reprogrammed to function as brains and not as taxi meters. In the beginning a brain was created to be a brain, not a taxi meter.

6. *Taking the day off just before you get sick.* The common cold and influenza do not get enough respect these days. We expect our doctors to hand us a shot of penicillin to keep us going, although the penicillin is not intended for a whole squadron of viruses. Antibiotics are no substitute for rest. Pain-killing drugs were not invented to be used so we can finish the present game with unbearable pain we have numbed with narcotics. As one wise physician said to me about pain killers: "Don't use them so you can add more duties to your day. Use rest to reduce pain inasmuch as possible and is workable." Therefore, as I have already noted, one way of being considerate of colleagues at work is *not* to come to work when running fevers. Another way to be considerate of ourselves is to take a day of rest *before* we get a cold or the flu rather than after it has downed us for the count of nine.

Free-time Vacations

So much for vacations on the job. We have avoided the realities of free-time vacations long enough. This is my propensity and it is yours. We wait until either the time, the number of pages, or the money has run out and then think of free-time vacations. I would choose to divide the kinds of vacations into what I hope can be built into an "International Classification of Vacations." That is how global I can get. How global can you get? This will take some doing because vacations are eccentric and idiosyncratic to the nth degree. I will start it, and you and your friends can continue to develop this classification of vacations in free time, apart from the job. I will list my classification and will leave some additional spaces for your contribution to the international classification. By all means send me a copy of your list, plus any challenge of my list so that this can be a collaborative undertaking.

1. *Doing work you personally want to do regardless of whether it fits your job or not?* It may or may not be job-related. I asked a psychiatric resident what his definition of vacation was. He replied, "A vacation is a batch of work that you do in between two other large segments of work." The difference in this batch of work is that you are doing what you yourself have chosen to do and not what someone else expects of you. For example, I would like to read a long, technical volume on a particular kind of illness. My supervisor said to me that that was the kind of work one does on one's vacation!" I can resonate with him. I like to visit libraries and book stores and browse to my heart's content. I have had this habit since I was a little boy and would walk a couple miles to get to browse in the library. It is a very pleasant and renewing experience that I rarely get the chance to do on the job. I recall being on a commission of the Association of Theological Schools for the awarding of grants for sabbatical leaves to faculty members in schools of the Association. A person applying had to justify his or her need of money by such things as needing it to travel to and from a foreign country and out of his or her own culture. One man wanted to stay home and visit his own library of his own school on an uninterrupted basis. He said in his application: "I know that one should go to a foreign country. I can justify that by saying that the library on our campus is a foreign country to me!"

2. *A Do-it-yourself Community Project Vacation.* Some people use vacation time to enjoy an unusual kind of diversionary work. A group of people who know and enjoy each other's company get together to help one of them to accomplish a task that is too heavy or extensive for one man or woman to do in a day. Rural women even now have "quiltings" in which a number of them get together to "put in" and "quilt" a quilt. Rural men will often get together for a barn-

raising. In connection with this just yesterday I visited a home where a group of men had gathered together to put a new roof on the house of one of them. A feast of food had been prepared and it was sort of a celebration that more than two-thirds of the job was completed between 8:30 A.M. and noon. Many times this kind of work-use of free times takes on the quality of a generous act toward someone who is helpless or vastly bereaved or both. I recall a group of graduate students who got together to sell the library of a fellow student who had died both suddenly and tragically. His wife had asked that the books be sold. They went further; they placed books of their own that were not in use into the sale. They got together nearly $2,000 for the widow of their fallen comrade. Students at the Presbyterian and Southern Baptist Theological Seminaries in Louisville became a massive work force helping neighbors of the schools whose houses were badly damaged by the tornado of April 3, 1974.

3. *Health Defense and Repair Vacations.* Every so often even a good ship needs to go into dry-dock for overall inspection, repair, and refitting. A fine piece of machinery has to have periodic maintenance overhauls. The human organism is the finest mechanism we know about. People on a job tend to understand it when a colleague has to go to his or her physician. Last year I took a health defense and repair vacation. I took one whole week having different systems of my body checked out, and if need be repaired. A recurrently bothersome right knee, a chronic sinusitis, an old back injury, etc. were on the list. I did find it time consuming. However, it was of such a helpful nature that I have had much less discomfort in the past year than for many years previous. This will take a weekend, plus a couple days, probably Monday and Thursday of a work week. Then the Friday can be taken off for sheer goofing off or a long weekend, plus a couple days, probably Monday and Thursday or a work week. Then the next Friday can be taken off also for sheer goofing off or a long weekend vacation of some other kind. In between, one can work Tuesday and Wednesday and stay in touch with one's duties. However, I would advise that one take his or her own choice of

reading to the doctors' waiting rooms, unless one just has great curiosity as to what last year's national magazines read like one year later.

An organized example of the health defense and repair kind of vacation is the program of Health Hazard Appraisal at the Methodist Hospital in Indianapolis, Indiana, under the leadership of Dr. Ken Reid. A man and his wife leave their work and come to the medical center for a thorough two-day physical examination and for counseling on an individual and group basis as to how their work and way of life are contributing to or militating against their best health. As far as I know, this is a unique program. The couple who waits until something serious goes wrong has to spend many times this much time and money without choice or enjoyment. I do not know of another such program, but it's certainly worthy of emulation.

4. *The "All-true-lovers' Festival" Vacation.* Tender loving care, undivided attention, and freedom from responsibility of work outside and in the home are some of the ingredients that make for a husband-wife festival of the renewal of their sexual life together. Many parents with young children go for weeks without saying a sentence to each other that is not interrupted by a child. To get a baby-sitter, to make a reciprocal agreement on child care with another couple, to arrange for relatives to let the children visit is necessary to couples who want to get away from the demands of life at home and at work. This can be done. It takes some planning and effort. These vacations are possible on a weekend or at best on a long weekend of three days. Even after the children are grown and out of the home, the renewal of the love life of couples of any age can be memorably accomplished by a trip to a nearby state park, to an unusual community in easy driving distance of home, etc. I recall a beautiful November trip to a small German community in Frankenmuth, Michigan, which my wife and I made. She is deeply interested in interior decorations and Christmas decorations. Frankenmuth is a center for the creation of and manufacture of Christmas decorations. We

had excellent German food and freedom from crowds. Nature even co-operated and provided a light snow for the occasion.

5. *Working Vacations.* The Presidents of our country have coined the term, "working vacation"; or, at least their press officers have. The working vacation is, for ordinary citizens like you and me, such a thing as taking either your mate or your whole family with you in connection with some duty you have to accomplish. One of the advantages of couples whose children are grown and out of the home is that they can have more such vacations as these. For example, convention-going is usually built around this kind of motif. If one's own personal expenses are covered, then the additional expense of one's mate is not exorbitant. Old friends are met at these gatherings and a holiday atmosphere makes the rest of the tedium of the convention reasonably bearable. (Personally I hate conventions with a smiling passion.) If a vacation motif were not built into them, I daresay they would be sparsely attended if attended at all. Yet, for many couples who are on low salaries and tight budgets, this is a fringe benefit of the job that should be guarded jealously. Otherwise, they might never get a vacation.

The kind of working vacation I enjoy best is one in which I receive an assignment for one or, at the most, two days of work. Then the time before or after the meeting in which I work, or both, my wife and I can have as a time of our own for "getting lost" from the crowd, going to interesting places, etc. The work does two things: It takes the sting of guilt out of spending all that money on hotels and transportation; it pays for most of the vacation. If it can be done on a break-even basis, I like to think of this as a vacation in which we "forage off the land" rather than our budget. In fact, I enjoy "splurging" this kind of money on a vacation.

6. *Wanderschaft or "wandering" vacations.* Erik Erikson says that persons, especially adolescent persons, need a psychological moratorium from the demands of life before they make the great decisions of life. I would agree, but I would not restrict it to adolescents. I see many middle-aged persons today who need just that. They need an extended break from

the unremitting pressures of life to go into their own personally chosen kind of wilderness to think life through, to reflect
on the larger issues of life and to get a broad-gauged perspective on the meaning of their lives without the rattle of other
people's opinions to confuse them. They need time to let their
minds wander until they find their own sense of direction.
Sometimes this can be arranged between job changes. Other
times it can be a leave of absence. At even other times it can
be a sabbatical kind of experience, or it can be supported by
grants, bequests, gifts. If a person is making too much money
to please him or her when income tax time comes to pass, then
this could possibly be a way of cutting one's income at a time
when refreshing insights, new energy, and abundance of time
are more valuable to the survival of the best in life than is
money.

Recently a university president took this kind of vacation in
a remarkably unique way. He chose to get completely out of
the role of a university president and try to make his own way
in the world working as a day laborer and blue collar worker.
The encounter he had with himself was a revolution in his
view of himself and the world in which he lives.

A whole generation or two of young people got this kind of
wanderlust in the sixties and early seventies. They went "on
the bum." Just as I have begun this paragraph, I finished a
conversation with a fifteen-year-old girl who says that she
wants next year to "go out West." With a faraway look in her
eyes, she fantasizes of how easy it will be. She said that her
parents did not mind and that they would be rid of her. That,
she said, would make them happy. Yet, before the conversation she was wondering just what she was going to do in the
long run with her life. She said that she just had to solve the
need to be free from being tied down before she would make
any sense to herself or be of any use to the world.

Adult and youth alike feel the need to get away, to forget,
to wander. That is the most consistent definition of a vacation
I get from persons of all ages. The tragedy of this is that the
big cities and the wildernesses are both so commercialized
that achieving this is a very different thing from the dream

that it will be. Yet the need for solitude is at the core of it. Alfred North Whitehead spoke of a person's religion when he said that religion is what a person does with his/her solitude. The ancient contemplatives spent their time in the desert. Moses, Jesus, Paul, St. Anthony, and many others made their great decisions and struggled with the big temptations of their inner beings in the desert. The need for that is only thinly obscured in modern life. The tragedy is that many people today never find that in life until they have to go to a hospital or be confined by a non-killing illness for an extended length of time.

7. *Adventure-risk Vacations.* I read about persons who like to "shoot the rapids" of the great rivers of the West. I see examples of this on television. Others like to go on wild-game hunts in Africa. Others like to try to learn to hang glide or sky dive. These are what I call adventure vacations. I can't leave this kind of vacation out of the nomenclature just because I cannot understand it or "get into" the kind of thinking that produces it. Our older son is put together this way. His scuba diving adventures, mountain climbing, and experiments with parachuting are just a few of the less-risky things he has done, much less some of those he has thought of often. Yet, it is impulses like these that have opened up the unexplored recesses of the earth and the universe for him and for many others, whether I can get into the kind of thinking or not. It is a historic kind of idea of a vacation.

I know a dynamic singles group in a large Southwest city. While on a speaking engagement in their city, I was invited to an evening's "at ease" conversation with them. They told me of their summer vacation which they had shared together as a group. They had ridden in station wagons to Miami. There they rented a sail boat that was large enough to provide bunks and hammocks and cooking space for them. They spent the month cruising to the Caribbean islands and managing the navigation between stops. They did deep-sea fishing, encountered a storm at sea, tested their abilities to assess wind currents for the sail adjustments, and negotiated with harbor officials who did not know them. They all returned safely and in good health.

I listened to their story with an envious sense of awe wishing that I had been there. Yet, I wondered if I could have been that adventurous. I am sure, though, most of them wondered that, too. That is the main part of an "adventure vacation."

8. *The Vacation in One's Own Home.* A vacation that I have enjoyed with my family has been one in which we stay at home. We decide to travel out into the city or the surrounding three-state area during the days to places of interest that are not so far that we cannot get back home in the evening. We take in entertainments in the city of Louisville in the evenings when we do not travel too far during the day. We always come back and sleep in our own beds. This frees up enough money that would be spent on lodging elsewhere to enable us to splurge a bit on other things in our own environment. If we want to be free of the impact of the demands of others on us, we have solved the problem of the telephone. We learned from one of our friends who is a physician that a button can be installed on the telephone so that it rings but we do not hear it. Thus we are not conscience stricken by not answering the phone. We do not hear it.

The irony of spending the vacation at home is when persons who themselves have the same university holidays I do call and say that they have the week off, have some extra time, and would like to schedule conferences with me about their work! I simply reply that I have the holidays off, too, and am on vacation and will be glad to see them when we are both back from our holidays. Such responses, of course, do not cover dire emergencies, but the essence of working in an emergency atmosphere is to "swap off" time with colleagues and "cover" for one another when on vacation—a grand tradition in the medical profession that could well be adapted to other lines of work. The physicians work in groups and "cover" each other's emergencies when the other is getting a few days of rest and recreation.

Address your messages to me at: Author Mail, Doubleday &

Company, Inc., 245 Park Avenue, New York, New York 10017. Now that I have listed my part of the international classification of vacations, please add yours on this page and explain them. Then, if you will, mail a copy of your list to me.

Why We Do Not Take Vacations

With all the possibilities for a culturally sanctioned kind of lazy use of free time, why is it, then, that so many people have such a hard time taking a vacation? I hear a great deal about mandatory retirement, but I have rarely heard of mandatory vacations. The Union Theological Seminary in New York City has a ritual for requiring their staff to take a vacation. They change the locks on all doors and lock the whole place up tightly. They inform everyone to be out of the buildings by a certain deadline. But they are the exception. The rule is to compliment persons who retire for "never having taken a vacation" during their tenure. Slavery is often mistaken for "devotion to duty."

We have many reasons for avoiding taking a vacation. Not the least among these reasons is the commercialization of vacation times. Prices are "In Season" and "Off Season" in vacation areas. Add this to the stubborn cultural leaning to want more money than more time off, and the excessive expense of vacations is a doubly reinforced reason for not taking them. The sense of guilt at spending so much money that you do not *have* to spend, but choose to spend, becomes epidemic among persons considering a vacation.

The work addict is likely not to want to take a vacation because he or she dreads the "withdrawal symptoms" from work. No positive addiction like an earned right to laziness has taken the place of the old negative addiction to work unless the addict has had a real conversion from his negative addiction. Underneath all this is a basic sense of worthlessness apart from work. As one work addict says: "The only thing I am any good for is to work and make money. I don't deserve having a lot of money spent on myself." This blends into a sort of depression that is painful enough on vacation to condition the person to avoid the whole thing as being more trouble than it is worth.

Some of the symptoms of withdrawal from work and solutions for them are:

1. Delaying the time for beginning a vacation a day at a time: "We thought we were going on vacation today, but Daddy had some more work at the office. Mother had to finish cleaning the house."

The solution to this is to leave the job and the house on a "walk out" basis. Procrastination on leaving for vacation is a fear of "not finishing" everything. You are not dying. You are merely going on vacation!

2. Physical symptoms emerge. Some persons with pains from old injuries, spinal surgery, arthritis, etc. will discover that this pain becomes intense from "letting down" on vacation. Others will develop gastro-intestinal symptoms. Others will have increased breathing difficulties. Usually these symptoms will be most evident for the first three days. Adequate medical consultation may call for some appropriate medication. Forced extra sleep for these three days will break the cycle. This is why driving long distances the first days of a vacation are great deterrents to vacations. If the distance is over two hundred miles, I like to stop the first night for a good dinner in a restful location, spend the night, and sleep late the next morning before tackling the long end of the journey.

3. Family conflict is another symptom of withdrawal symptoms. Remember, many families work in a separate place for each family member. They often ride in different cars. On vacation, they converge into one car. Stress escalates. The irritability, sense of physical discomfort and distractibility of the work-addicted person are all increased in the bickering. Already having had trouble "tearing away from the job," he/she is likely to become enraged and call the whole vacation off. That is the safer thing to do. The hazardous thing done more often is to drive a car, with the whole family in it, in a state of anger that may escalate to rage and cause an accident. The so-

lution to this is not to drive in a car when in a severe state of anger or rage. Instead of calling the whole vacation off, simply say, "I am in a bad state of mind. All of us are upset. Let's wait an hour or two and get our moods back into shape. It is dangerous to drive this way."

One of the hindrances to vacations is the way in which people are "duty bound" to spend time off with relatives. For many, this is a joy, a celebration, and a time of fulfillment. I suspect for many more it is a time of depression, rehashing old family conflicts, and "doing social work" on multi-problem conditions in families. Many people would rather work a whole week than to visit relatives for a day. Yet they feel compelled to do this "duty." I assess these issues regularly in counseling with patients and counselors. A whole research project is hurting to be done here.

Work addicts, also, are often poorly understood by their families whom they tend to indulge in meeting all *their* wants. Their families are so accustomed to enjoying the fruits of the work addict's labors, that they take the money-getter for granted and have little time for simply being with and seeking to understand the feelings of their goose that lays the golden eggs. Seeing himself as a "goose," teaches the family to see the same thing—a goose.

The critical issue at base, however, is that the insulation of work relieves the person who cannot make laziness work for him of the necessity for intimacy and forthright conversation and candor with one's own flesh and blood. If a vacation is likely to push us face to face with ourselves and we fear this, then it is all the more likely to shake the balance that keeps a hyperactive family flying in every direction rather than enjoying the pleasure of each other's company. Consequently, even in the planning of a vacation procrastination may let the whole thing go by default.

The main need, then, is to consider what kind of vacation fits best and to do so before income tax time each year.

CHAPTER 4

The Hazards of Laziness

Y ou might be saying to yourself, "Anybody with any common sense at all knows that some people are just plain lazy. They work themselves to death getting out of work. They are not worth the salt they eat nor the gunpowder it would take to shoot them. They are just plain lazy, no account, and trifling."

If you have never heard or thought this assessment of a lazy person, you will if you listen closely to others. Do not write this estimate off as worthless. When I hear you or anyone else say this I learn that laziness is a potent hazard in human relationships. If a form of behavior can pull such intense feelings out of other people, then the hazards of laziness are multiple, to say the least. If laziness is to be taken in therapeutic doses, then the hazards of addiction to laziness are as great as the hazards of addiction to work. To say this to you is to warn you. If you are among those who think that laziness comes in "just plain" forms, you are underestimating its power to mess up human relationships. Laziness as an addiction is subtle and devastating. For example, reread the first paragraph of this page. See for yourself what kinds of emotions go with it: anger, exasperation, disgust, despair, violence! Any kind of behavior that can stir up the cup of human feelings like that is not "just plain." Laziness can be loaded with hazards. What are some of the hazards of laziness?

Do You Procrastinate Until Your Friends
Lose Their Cool?

The first hazard of laziness is putting off doing what you have promised others to do. Procrastination is an effortless way of making them angry. This anger is more intense in your own family members. Your wife, or husband, and your children may complain that you are putting them at the bottom of the list of those for whom you promise to do things. When you do promise them something, you never "get around to it." You, in turn, lay a guilt load on them and say, "Well, I would get around to it if you did not nag me so much." When you accuse them of nagging they do a slow burn and keep their mouths shut. Finally, in exasperation, they blow up and a shouting match ensues. What a ragged state of human existence! You go to work the next day feeling sorry for yourself, feeling genuinely misunderstood and unappreciated, and drag through the day of work. Procrastination is not only the thief of time; it is the armed robber of human fellowship.

Promises lightly made are poorly kept. One reason you and I do not "get around to" doing what we have promised is that we have entered into the promise situation lightly and unwisely. I recall a situation in which I had promised a colleague of mine to organize a small fund-raising luncheon for which he and his institution would pay. I deferred making the plans for three or four days after I had made the promise. Several other events pressed in upon my schedule and time erased the promise from my memory. On the late afternoon of the day the luncheon was supposed to be, my colleague called me. He was justifiably offended. I was horribly embarrassed. I apologized profusely. He forgave graciously.

As I sought to understand why I would make such a big blunder, I realized I had promised the impossible to the man. I had committed other people's time at a time of day they do not have any free time. I had made an unwise promise. I had not thought through what I was doing. I wanted the other person's approval so much that I promised that which I could not fulfill. In the end I earned his anger instead. Promises! Promises! Promises!

Such ill-thought-through promises underlie much procrastination. The one experience I have just described burned me enough that I learned from it. Procrastination is not a way of life for me. It may be a way of life for you. You may be addicted to procrastination. You may be an administrator who has many people asking you for things—perquisites of their office, promotions, pay raises, etc. They may ask you for these things in the hall while you are on your way some place. They may press harder by making an appointment and visiting you in your office. They may follow this up in a written memorandum. They may resort to having their particular division of your institution or company to vote to ask you for the coveted reward. In all instances, you may defer making a decision. You do not say yes. You do not say no. You do nothing. Thus, your own inaction begins to work against you. The person or persons may be able to take a clean "No!" from you more easily than this procrastination shot through with indecision. Finally, you may begin to wonder why this person becomes hostile, belligerent, and somewhat irrational. You have never done anything to him. You have been courteous, smiled, complimented his children, and even had him out to your favorite club for lunch. What on earth could this person be angry about when you have been so "nice"? Could it be that you express your anger by procrastinating?

You have made your colleague angry without really trying. You have expressed your own anger by the things you do *not* do. Thus your own inaction—or laziness—has begun to work against you rather than for you. You can make your laziness work for you by being decisive, by doing something even if it frustrates others. They can stand the frustration better than they can the indecision. By the time you have put off a decision the twentieth time, you could have made it and used the time you saved to loaf, enjoy the leaves on the tree outside your office, or even go home and take a nap.

Yet, you may, upon having had this called to your attention, prefer to continue to express your disdain for your colleagues by passive-aggressive games of procrastination. If so, do not be surprised some day if enough of them band together and present your superiors with charges against you of administrative inaction, administrative harassment, and administrative incompetence. Do not be amazed if the personnel office presents you with a stack of "exit interview" complaints against you. Employees quit. They get tired of wasting time trying to budge you out of indecision and inaction in order to get a decent day's work done. They go home and goof off happily on their own time. They told it like it is on exit interviews.

Both editors and authors of books, articles, etc. are well acquainted with the ways in which procrastination becomes an editor-author or author-editor laziness game that works against rather than for the experience of creative publishing. Authors will say, "That editor kept my manuscript for three months before I heard from him. The ideas were beginning to grow beards by the time I got a publisher response!" Editors will say, "He had a deadline that he put off seven times. The first two were for strong reasons. The last five became less and less convincing." Worse than this, "We signed a contract with him and paid him a modest royalty advance three years ago. We have never heard from him since. He doesn't answer our mail." Meanwhile back at the university, students in the senior class are advising freshmen to laugh in class when the professor tells them about his new manuscript that has been accepted by the publishers!

One antidote for such an overdose of laziness in the form of procrastination can be found in eagerness for approval that prompts you and me to promise to do things that do not really fit our deepest aspirations in life. We are trying to be somebody else other than ourselves. Saying "No!" would demand that you or I stand up and be counted as a person who enjoys talking to students more than we do writing books, articles, etc. You might even precipitate a movement within academic circles of valuing students more than publishing books. Then, instead of spending the weekend writing (for there is no time in the work week provided for that kind of work), you might spend it on a ski trip with a group of your students. You really enjoy teaching skiing, but there is no room for it in the curriculum! This makes laziness work for you instead of letting it "do you in" with a procrastination game with publishers.

The only way I can "get into" the forces that would cause an editor to procrastinate is by likening their task to my own task of grading student papers. I graded papers as a student assisting professors for seven years in undergraduate and graduate school. Who *enjoys* reading the same material forty-three times? I don't. A set of papers to grade is, therefore, my greatest temptation to procrastination. Rather than have the fast growing monster of this temptation taking up more and more room in the small quarters of my mind, I grade the papers the two evenings after I get them. I return them in seventy-two hours. The students are pleased that I have "insured prompt service," I can use the papers as teaching devices and for correction of my own failures of communication with students. The underlying motive, however, was originally to get the temptation to procrastinate out of the house of my mind.

Editors may have the same problem with author manuscripts that I have described in grading student papers. The editor's task is actually that of "grading" the production of authors. This calls for decision making. Indecision on the part of the editor, or simply the unpleasantness of telling an author that the material must be revised or rejected may make it easier to turn to more pleasant tasks and leave this one undone until tomorrow, tomorrow, and tomorrow. Procrastination rides again and confuses the author-editor relationship. Anxiety and hostility take the place of laughter as "just plain laziness" reveals itself as a tool of indecision and anger. The solution? Bite the bullet. Make a few unpopular decisions. Take the next day off for fun and games. You have earned two days' pay today.

Does Your Fear of Failure Keep You from Doing Things?

A second hazard of laziness is that you will permit your fear of failure to keep you from doing what you would like to do. If you never try a particular job, you can never accuse yourself of having failed. You simply never got around to it. You substitute ruminating about what might happen if you really tried a given job, for specific actions to see what would happen. I have a fear of failure as a swimmer. The consequences of such a failure would be disastrous: I would drown. I have repeatedly tried to learn to swim. My sons and my wife, all of whom are excellent swimmers, have cautiously tried to teach me. I am unable to learn this skill because of an overriding fear of failure. Other people have like fears about driving an automobile. I would have the same fears about piloting a plane. I suspect that such skills as public speaking, writing, surgery, diamond-cutting, etc. are a few examples of tasks not undertaken because of the fear of failure.

Such tasks fall into two groups, however: Some of them are a part of the work you and I have chosen. Others are not. If I had chosen to be a rescue squad leader on a river patrol, my fear of failure as a swimmer would stare me in the face daily. If you are a salesperson who is expected to drive the company car in your work, the fear of driving an automobile would plague your everyday activities. If a medical student fears failure in surgery, the fear may be so overriding that he would best be advised to choose a specialty such as physical medicine, internal medicine, or psychiatry—in which cutting procedures are not required. Facing up to your fears is one way of accepting your limitations before they immobilize you into total inaction, or get you into the wrong job.

Another sphere in which the fear of failure is one of the hazards of laziness is the school classroom. You may be the father or mother of a son or daughter who is always in trouble at report card time. He or she comes home with bad grades. You get uptight because of your own ambitions for the young person. Ambition seems to be somewhere else for your offspring. You have ruled out several things. First, you thought he was dumb; therefore, you took the young person to a private psychologist who found him to be of at least normal intelligence. Second, you may also have learned that the child's talents are different from yours. You cannot expect the child to be an achiever in the same areas you are. Third, you may have been advised by the psychologist to "get off the kid's back." You are asked to become more relaxed about the school performance of your child. The psychologist may tell you that in a testing situation your child will "freeze" up on exams. Fears take over. Inaction and non-performance cause the fear of failure to become a fact.

Now, take a close look at your own way of performing. You may exude confidence. You "knocked the top out of" every exam or test you ever took. When you got out of school, you became a successful actor in the drama of the work world. You made all your competitors cringe with anxiety as they sought to outdo you. Anywhere you go now, you are a hard act to follow. This is no secret to your child. It has been his companion since before the child learned to talk. You indeed *are* a hard act to follow! Your son or daughter "gives up." You try all the harder to make your success hereditary. It will not work. Then you discover that your child is proficient and interested in things that are foreign to you. You resist the temptation to "put down" these interests. You notice that the youngster is highly proficient in things you would be afraid to tackle. He is offsetting the fear of failure in *your* territory by feverish courage in his own territory. You are fortunate indeed if this happens, if you can affirm your own children's uniqueness, and if you have the relaxation to be open and learn of their world.

The Sidney B. Coulter Library
Onondaga Community College
Rte. 173, Onondaga Hill
Syracuse, New York 13215

The more common outcome of such cases, however, is that the underachiever is "written off" as a bright but lazy person. The child may be given a sense of inferiority and fear in the face of a world of industry and achievement. Laziness is the marketplace label placed on that child. "Just plain lazy and good for nothing" is a harsher name. The young person, however, has let himself get trapped in a failure outlook as a way of being a person in his own right. As one third grader said to his father who had urged him to talk with some of the other children and ask how they went about making good grades, "I could never do that. If I learned how they do it, I would be them. I've got to learn how I do it so that I can be me." That boy was industrious about many things; only occasionally did these things coincide with what the teacher and his father wanted. Daniel Blaine, a psychiatrist in the student health program of Harvard, has said, "What is so commonly termed laziness, lack of will power, or a poor attitude is at heart a stubborn resentfulness expressed by a stubborn refusal to do anything demanded by authority." (*Youth and the Hazards of Affluence*, New York: Harper & Row, 1966, p. 30.) In the instance cited here, the little boy was challenging the authority of both his father and that of his peer group of fellow students. He was already working at his own uniqueness. The hazard of his "laziness" or non-performance would be that he would suffer isolation and loneliness by his stubbornness and fear of failure according to the standards of his teachers, his peers, and his father. His hope lay in having a father who would "join up" with him in his search for his uniqueness, his own territory, and his separate identity. As William Glasser has aptly said, "*Thus, those who fail in our society are lonely. In their loneliness, they grope for identity, but to the lonely the pathways to success are closed.*" (*Schools Without Failure*, New York: Harper & Row, 1969, p. 17.) Hopefully, the schools themselves can respond to the lonely student. Certainly, companionship the parent provides the son or daughter with an additional pathway of love and self worth.

Do Your Fantasies of Great Achievement Keep You from Ordinary Accomplishment?

Fantasy is at one and the same time a source of creativity and a hazardous source of inaction. You can become addicted to fantasy. Do you substitute dreaming for action as a steady habit? I am not trying to stop you from dreaming. Without dreams of greatness, greatness does not often happen. I am asking you about overdoses of fantasy that turn inaction into laziness—a hazard. Are you such a perfectionist in your expectations of "the whole thing" that you will not settle for a reasonable approach to your dreams? In turn, does this "perfectionism" make it easy for you to weasel out of the responsibilities that opportunities at hand give you?

An example of this inaction is Thomas Wolfe's account of the waiter in a restaurant where Wolfe was eating. The waiter serving him kept wanting to talk to him. Wolfe encouraged him to do so. The man cleared his throat. He looked cunningly around "to make sure that he was in no danger of being overheard and that his priceless secret would be safe." Wolfe says that the waiter then "bent over and coyly whispered that he had in his brain for several years 'a Great Idea for a Story.'" The waiter assured him that as a reward for Wolfe's supervision and sponsorship of the "Great Idea for a Story," he would cut him in on the profits, movie rights, etc. which would "be simply staggering." Wolfe said that he would like to hear it. He fixed a grin on his face to look interesting. He said that the "Great Idea for a Story" would "make Cecil B. Demille in his most fantastic moments look like a stern realist." The waiter assured Wolfe that the story had been given to him by a Greek who insisted that the story had a real basis in fact. It was "all about 'a dame in Assyria' and her love affair." She was rich. Her old man locked her up on top of his thirty-story house. Her boyfriend climbs up the thirty stories each night to play his banjo to her. The old man dies. The couple marry. The husband turns out to be a "booze hound" and to run around "with a bunch of hot blondes." He deserts the woman he has married, and the woman spends much money trying to find him. She finally falls on a great scheme of her own to open up the "swellest night club that anybody ever heard of in Assyria." She began to give free booze to all the "booze hounds" with the hope of finding her husband among them. When they all gathered, she went downstairs. As luck would have it, there her husband was first in line. The peak of the story is that she has a veil on and he does not recognize her. She challenges him to come upstairs and prove to her that he really is a booze hound. They get upstairs and she takes the veil off!

Wolfe asked him, "Then what? What happens then?" The waiter was disgusted and said, "Then nothing. That's all: she got him back, see? And isn't it a wow?"

Wolfe said that more far-fetched and preposterous the story, the less it has to do with life, the better the "Great Idea for a Story" appears to the fantasies of persons like the waiter. He says that all the while the human drama of a dozen stories is taking place right around the waiter: People "coming in and out; the other waiter who is a communist who argues violently for revolution with any customer who will talk with him; the little waitress who has had an illegitimate child a few months ago and has put it into a home; and other human things and episodes like this—the whole weave and shift and interplay of life and comedy and tragedy that goes on in a place like this. And all the time the waiter is earnestly telling this preposterous fable—his 'Great Idea for a Story'—to the customer." (Adapted from *The Letters of Thomas Wolfe*, edited by Elizabeth Nowell, Charles Scribner's Sons.)

The advantage the fantasy provides is the freedom from the necessity of doing anything at all about it. The waiter kept on waiting on tables, I assume. He did not become a writer. Yet, commitment to causing the "Great Idea for a Story" to make sense to other people was not there. When Wolfe did not get the point of the whole fantastic story, the waiter was disgusted. In grandiose contempt, he patronizingly let Wolfe in on the big secret: the "Assyrian dame" got her boozer back. Along with his "Great Idea for a Story," the waiter could look down with disgust on his customer for not "getting the point." He seemed to refuse to populate a world that had in it only mortals like Wolfe.

You may know persons like the waiter. You may have a humorous sense of kinship with him. I have a fantasy of being able to meet all my financial obligations by writing. I know in reality that other people have starved and neglected their families as they entertained this fantasy. I know that my compromise with reality in behalf of my fantasy is that writing as I do now is a "world of my own" from which I can draw realistic satisfaction in addition to dreaming about it. I can make the difference between a comfortable and a more-than-adequate income by writing. Yet, I have had opportunity to spend as much as a whole year at nothing but writing. The writing seemed to be less satisfying than writing in the midst of the day's work in my job at a medical school. Writing seems to be a rest along the way from the burning heat of the day's work and from the burdens of the day. The fantasy of being able to spend full time writing and to make my full income that way is really one way of excusing myself from the hours spent at a typewriter—as I am now. I refuse to "give up" my fantasy. I refuse to "give in to" my fantasy, either. I choose to enjoy my fantasy. Wouldn't it be great to have a beach house on a sparsely populated strand of the seaside? The fantasy of a dyed-in-the-wool workaholic like me is to be a beach bum who writes perfect lines—for a half hour a day! To give in to that fantasy would be to do away with whatever creativity I have as a writer. To give up that fantasy would be to forget how to laugh at interruptions, to enjoy the playful in life. It would be to become a *complete* bore.

Your fantasies may be considerably different from mine. I encourage you to know what your fantasies are, to enjoy them, to laugh at yourself with them, and to make them a form of play in and of themselves. Yet, are you locked into dreamy laziness that hazards your own relationships to other people through your fantasies? Have your fantasies become something for which other people should be expected to pay? Are you addicted to your fantasies to such an extent that you expect others to support your habit? If so, the signs of toxic hazard show in your parasitism.

Toxic fantasies have sabotaged the life and happiness of some valuable persons I have known. A few concrete examples are representative of many persons and not "case histories" anyone. In all instances, the fantasy of the "Great Idea . . ." is characteristic. For example, I know persons in their fifties who perceive their task to be that of philosophers. They speak of Spinoza, Hegel, Kierkegaard, and Whitehead as if these persons were peers. They spin one abstraction upon another. They remind you of the man who said he shingled his house during such a dense fog that he did not know when he came to the edge of the roof. He did not fall either. He just kept nailing the shingles to the fog. Thus, these persons' philosophy was so abstract that they fantasied that the fog itself held them up. Yet, they never held a job after they graduated from university. They were always "about" to land a prestigious teaching position in an Ivy League university. This never came to pass. In the meanwhile, they were living at the full expense of their aging but wealthy parents who for decades have spoken of them as "good with books" but as lazy and having no common sense. I often have gotten the uneasy feeling that they were simply waiting until their parents died. Then they could live on the inheritance. They would never have to make any commitment or share any durable responsibility. Their fantasy of the "big break" keeps them anesthetized to this reality.

Such a state of dream fantasy seems to be more nearly normative in many adolescents. Regardless of how normative it may be, similar abrasion with other people takes place as at any age. The youth feels he can do anything in the world. He can indulge in wild flights of imagination, soaring speculations, incredible adventures. He knows no limits in fantasy and accepts grudgingly any limits in reality. A young girl of eighteen sits at a table in the women's apparel section of a boutique. She dreams of owning her own boutique. She dreams of being married to an outstanding man. All of this happens in an instant of time in her fantasy. Neither time, space, money, or decision are anything to worry about now. Yet time, space, money, parental limits, moral decisions, etc. come in upon her. She then faces the reality of commitment and the slowness of growth in realistically achieving a secure marriage and a "boutique of her own." Another adolescent young woman toys with the idea of a patienthood in a hospital rather than come to terms with her fantasy that she was an artist whom no one could possibly understand. A young man sees himself as a celebrated guitarist. He feels that to take mundane work to support himself while he gets his "big break" as a recording artist would be a compromise of his "artistic integrity." He is less demanding, however, than his counterpart, who also married and became a father of two children, expecting his parents to support him and his family while he pursues his musical career.

The toxicity levels of laziness in such instances as these teach a sort of respect for laziness as a complicated chemistry of behaviors in persons. Examined closely, laziness and its capacity for toxic parasitism in human life cannot be underestimated with impunity to those doing the estimate. In the fantasy life unbounded you and I and those to whom we are related become prone to sickness ". . . with the pale cast of thought, and enterprises of great pitch and moment with this regard their currents turn awry, and lose the name of action." (William Shakespeare, *Hamlet, The Prince of Denmark*, Act III, Scene 1, ll. 85–88.)

Does Your Distrust of Others Keep You from Being a Dependable Worker?

Being a dependable worker is an inherent part of any responsible job. If you are not dependable, you are called lazy. Your fellow workers pick up the work for you. They say of you that you "want a job with all the work picked out of it." Arriving at the job late, persistently being absent, taking longer than agreed-upon lunch breaks, and not doing work assigned on time earn you the part of being a lazy, good-for-nothing who cannot be counted on to do anything. The immediate reaction of fellow workers is that you think you are a privileged character. Who do you think you are, they ask? If your superior or employer permits you to get away with this undependability and dumps your work on your fellow workers, then you are considered a "privileged character" who can get away with anything. Your employer may be simply afraid to confront you, to demand equal responsibility of you, or certainly to discharge you. You may be an "equal opportunity" employee who, if discharged, might charge your employer with discrimination against women, against blacks, against a myriad of other ethnic groups, or against people above the age of forty-five. You may be a relative of the supervisor's boss. You may be in a special category for many reasons and not just one. The result is the same: Your fellow workers hate your guts. Why should you get preferential treatment, they ask.

All of this happens on the outside of you. Meanwhile, let me guess a little about what is happening within your own thinking. You may well have taken the job you have all the while feeling distrustful of both your employer and your fellow employees. You could not trust them enough to ask them if you did not know how to do a particular job you have never done before. You just tried to figure it out for yourself. Then you were stuck with it. You would lose face if you admitted that you did not know how to do the job that you assured them you could. They may well have been glad if you said, "I just thought I knew how to do this. I do not. Would you explain it to me?" Yet, to do this you would need to have a lot of confidence in their good will. If you are a new employee and belong to a minority group, you have the multiple hurdles erected by social prejudice in them toward you and in you toward them. You and they "walk on eggs" concerning what you say and do. If you go ahead and do the job wrong or leave it half done because you really did not know how to do it and were afraid to ask, then you will find it harder to get up in time to get to work on time the next day. In fact, it will be very easy to use any excuse to call in and say you cannot make it at all. Then absenteeism as well as tardiness is on your record. By this time, your actions are setting you up to cause your suspicions to come true. You have really not made any genuine commitment or obligation of yourself to these persons. They think you are lazy and unreliable. You distrust them. You do not respect them as persons, and you feel that they do not respect you as a person. Your distrust keeps you from obligating yourself to work. Your lack of obligation prompts you to goof off on the job, to come in late, to leave early, and to be increasingly more absent. You have now set yourself up for them to get angry at you, to punish you, to threaten you, and to kick you out. When these things actually happen, your distrust is confirmed and you can say, "See! I told you so!"

Why then can you not form durable ties to your fellow workpersons? Why do you shift from one job to another so often? The pattern we have just imagined as happening within your own thinking may give you some clues. You may be one of the oppressed minority group members. You may indeed have come into the hostile environment as "the last to be hired and the first to be fired." You are given few incentives or rewards at best. You may burn with resentment at the disadvantage placed on you by race, religion, sex, or national origin. You may have been written off as lazy and good-for-nothing just because of your race, religion, sex, national origin, or social class. You are not alone on those feelings.

You will be encouraged and feel understood by James Baldwin. Prior to the 1976 Presidential election he wrote a syndicated article for many newspapers. His comments made me take stock of my own attitudes about calling people lazy. He addresses his remarks to the then unknown "Bicentennial Candidate" for the Presidency of the United States. He said that he was looking for that candidate.

"My father before me, also looked for you, for a long while. He gave up, finally, and died in an asylum. Perhaps I use the word 'asylum' with some bitterness. My father was a big, strong, handsome, healthy black man, who liked to use his muscles, who was accustomed to hard labor. He went mad and died in bedlam because, being black, he was always 'the last to be hired, and the first to be fired.'

"He—we—therefore, spent much of our lives on welfare, and my father's pride could not endure it. He resented it, and eventually came to hate the people who had placed him in this condition and who did not even have the grace or the courage to admit it.

"My father was not stupid and, God knows, he was not lazy. But his condition, against which I watched him struggle with all the energy he had, was blamed on laziness: And his wife, who knew better, and his children (who didn't) were assured, merely by the presence of the welfare worker, of his un-worthiness. No wonder he died in an American asylum—and at the expense, needless to say, of the so victimized American taxpayer. (My father was also an American taxpayer, and he paid at an astronomical rate.)" James Baldwin's father would have immeasurable amounts of distrust of those for whom he worked and with whom he worked. Baldwin's father's situation was much like that of Malcolm X's mother. Malcolm X told his story to Alex Haley in his autobiography.

Malcolm X faced the crisis of trust, efficiency, and "laziness" in minority groups. His father was mysteriously killed in the streets of East Lansing, Michigan. Only the smallest of two small insurance policies paid off. Malcolm X says: "So there we were. My mother was thirty-four years old, with no hus-band, no provider, or protector to take care of her eight chil-dren. . . . My mother began buying on credit. My father had always been very strongly against credit. 'Credit is the first step back into slavery.' " His mother got jobs because she was very white in appearance. When employers found that she was a Negro, they fired her. Welfare was a humiliation to her and the children. She sought to remarry and was badly jilted by a man. Malcolm X says: ". . . he finally backed away from taking on the responsibility of those eight mouths to feed." His mother began to break away from the horrible realities of her responsibilities. Malcolm X says: "Eventually my mother

suffered a complete breakdown, and the court orders were
finally signed. . . . They took her to the State Mental Hospital at Kalamazoo. . . . My mother remained in the same hospital at Kalamazoo twenty-six years." The children became
wards of the state. "They looked at us as numbers and as a
case in their books, not as human beings. . . . My mother in
there was a statistic that didn't have to be, that existed because of a society's failure, hypocrisy, greed, and lack of
mercy and compassion." It was not until he and his siblings
were a part of the Black Muslims that they found ways and
means of rescuing their mother and caring for her themselves.
(*Autobiography of Malcolm X*, New York: Grove Press, 1964,
pp. 18–22.)

I find myself overwhelmed as a white person who has my
own particular share of distrust of Establishment industry,
business, and education hierarchies of power. I am in even
more agony to fathom what it is like to be a black person, an
Indian, a woman, or Jehovah's Witness in a hostile "nice" environment that has legal agenda of "equal opportunity" but a
personal agenda of fierce competition for power, control, and
job security. The sufferings of James Baldwin and his parents
and of Malcolm X and his parents make me aware of the pyr-
amids of distrust that are the legacy of members of disad-
vantaged groups. I grope for words to guide anyone whose
distrust sabotages your work into the most subtle hazard of
what you are often accused of—laziness. The advice and
counsel of a farm woman to her daughter is good for me and
good for you.

Robert Coles, a psychiatrist, portrays the plight of the so-
called "lazy," which is at heart a crisis of distrust, fear, and
courage. He quotes the farm woman who says, "Well, I told
my girl she's going to be a beautiful flower, and so she has to
fight off all the weeds—the people who don't care but for
their own selves. And I told her not to be a timid plant, because they die; and its no good to want to do something and
fail, and die . . . You have to stand up to the weeds . . . You
have to lick your fear and not be timid." (*Children of Crisis:
A Study of Courage and Fear*, Boston: Little, Brown and Co.,

1964, p. 379.) If you do "stand up to the weeds," you will lay
aside your distrust of your employer and fellow employees
long enough to let each one of them have a chance at being
trustworthy. You will value trustworthiness and dependability
scrupulously and not let dereliction of duty be an occasion for
others to call you lazy. You will not set yourself up to fail,
although trusting anyone makes you vulnerable to being hurt.
The risk is worth it. James Baldwin, Malcolm X, and many
others are evidence for believing this. In their vulnerability
they laid themselves open enough to give me a glimpse of
their inner world. I need this for empathy's sake. I cannot
safely trust someone who will not let me know them.
Delighted are both you and I when we get to know who we
are and form bonds of trust based on knowledge of each
other's hopes and dilemmas. Consequently, I hope that this
section of this book will prompt responses to what I have said.
You may know far more about what I am talking about here
than I do. I certainly hope so. I need all the understanding I
can get of the way fear and distrust sabotage your efforts to
avoid the hazards of laziness.

Do Helplessness and Hopelessness Paralyze You into Inaction or Laziness?

Another hazard of laziness springs up in the hopeless feelings
of the person who has the "can't do's." You may feel generally
helpless in the face of the expectations of work. If you are a
man who came to the ages of eighteen to twenty-seven during
the years of the Vietnam War, you may have felt intensely
helpless in planning either work or school. If you are a woman
of similar age, you may have felt helplessness in thinking with
your male siblings and/or your male friends about the meaning of both work and marriage. You were clamped into the
limbo of indecision by a military draft into an indecisive war.
If you are nearing or now facing retirement, you may feel that
your age has automatically made you useless, powerless, and

helpless. You have been "shelved" and shoved until you throw in the towel and don't want to do anything. If you have lost someone by death, you may have lost one of the major incentives to do your work, i.e., to make things pleasant for that deceased loved one of yours. The housewife quits cooking "just for herself"; the widower loses concern about his job. Whereas some people you know will deny the whole loss of someone by death by "flying into" ceaseless activity, you instead have become immobilized by your grief. You don't want to do anything. Even six months to a year after the death of your loved one, you are helpless to take an initiative, to launch any new efforts, or try anything old or new. You are likely to call yourself lazy. Your helplessness causes you to think you are "good for nothing." Others may get the same idea and impatiently say that if you would just get up and start doing things, you would find that you are not as helpless as you think. It is easier for them to say this than it is for you to do it, even though you admit that is so.

On the job you may have been pushed and shoved around in the political rat race of the company, the industry, or the institution and now are not "with" the decision makers or one of those "in power." These pushes and shoves cause the power situation to shift from time to time. Time was, you may be saying, that "your word went"; not so any longer. Nothing you do or say matters. You are helpless. You are facing one of the hazards of laziness: expressing your anger by no longer performing your job well. You are sad, indecisive, unable to act, making increasing demands on others. You feel worthless and guilty about not doing your duty. Your "get up and go" has got up and gone.

When other people around you perceive your inaction, they may load you with guilt by accusing you of incompetence, shirking your duty, and laziness. You are likely to agree with them because your own self-esteem has gotten so low that you have been saying these things to yourself. Your life may be full of situations in which you felt devoid of a sense of mastery and covered by feelings of helplessness. I would hope that you do not really believe what others are saying about

you and what you are saying to yourself. You are not as helpless as you think, nor are you devoid of power. In fact, nothing you could do would be as controlling and powerful over
others as just sitting down in the sand trap of your own helplessness. Such imbibing of inaction and helplessness becomes
a toxic form of laziness. You are in a position to react
differently.

Look critically at your behavior and ask yourself if this is
the best choice of an outlook on life available to you. Is it best
for the people you love? What positive advantage does your
assumed helplessness have on your community around you?
You can become involved with someone who will assume that
you are responsible and who can enable you to believe in your
abilities as much as that person does. You can get enough ob-
jectivity to understand what you are doing. You can do something about your own point of view. The first thing you must
decide is that your assumed helplessness is not working. The
second thing is to ask what effects you are trying to get out of
those around you, and how they are taking your protestations
that you are powerless to do anything about your situation.

Let's review the several hazards of laziness so that we can
see them as something of "one piece of cloth." The patterns
are so interwoven that it is impossible to tell when one hazard
ends and the other begins. The first hazard of laziness is procrastination as a passive aggressive tool of our anger. The second hazard of laziness is the paralysis caused by an intense
fear of failure. A third hazard of laziness is the fantasy of
great achievements that overdoses you into inaction. A fourth
hazard of laziness is a deep-seated distrust of all with whom
and for whom we work that keeps us from making any commitment to them in shared work. A fifth hazard of laziness is a
sense of helplessness that imperializes our outlook on life to
the exclusion of any other possible outlook on life.

These hazards are toxic in their effect upon your whole life,
not just upon your involvement in the work world. They kill
off interpersonal harmony between you and significant other

persons in your life. After having asked yourself the five questions I have posed, I hope that you will find resources in your own candid appraisal of your addiction to a pattern of inaction to cause you to make significant changes. You are able to do this with the encouragement I give you and that which others will probably give you at the sight of the first changes in you. If not, then I do think you are dealing with issues in your life serious enough for you to seek out a competent therapist who can enable you on a personal basis to deal with your passive aggressiveness, your fear of failure, your languid fantasy-formations, your distrust of those around you, and/or your despairing supposition of helplessness.

Laziness is a powerful form of human behavior. The emotions of anger, fear, love of fantasy, distrust, and despair derive their power from the boiler-room of human motivation. These forces can be made to work for you and to cease and desist from working against you. Their end result in laziness arrived at this point in no simple way. Laziness is neither simple nor weak. Therefore, harnessing your laziness into creative and away from hazardous directions is your ethical responsibility to yourself as a fully functioning person.

CHAPTER 5

*Being Lazy in
All Good Conscience*

Laziness is a matter of conscience. Even the person who never has a pang of conscience may have family members and friends who constantly moralize at him: "Have you no conscience at all being so lazy?" As I have been writing these chapters, I have talked with many individuals and groups about laziness. They think it strange that a confessed workaholic would become intrigued with being lazy. At least I am well defended against their moral condemnation of me. As we continue our conversations, they themselves become confessional and say, "Yes, but I feel so guilty when I goof off. My conscience gets the best of me for wasting time. I have so many things to be done. They hang over my head like a dark rain cloud that won't rain. I am uneasy and conscience stricken."

You not only have a right to laziness, you have a right to demand of me that I talk with you without beating the devil around the bush about your and my uneasy conscience when we have earned the right to laziness. Why do you have such a hard time "cashing in" on your days off from work to rest, play, make love, lie in the sun long enough that somebody warns you that you are about to blister, etc.? You are suffering from a bad conscience about being lazy, about doing nothing, about exercising your right to laziness. The ability to be lazy in all good conscience, then, is the huge impediment to a balance of rest with a reasonable amount of work. A bad conscience is a tyrant. A good conscience is a co-laborer. A good conscience is also a source of serenity, joyful play, and it enables us to dream creatively.

The Good Conscience of the Idle Person

You have heard it said that "the idle mind is the devil's workshop." The idle person, to tell the other half of the truth, *can* be doing a disciplined kind goodness. Some of the most difficult states of awareness you and I have to realize amounts to our simply being idle, *not* doing things. We do not get this attitude from Western culture. The Orientals have mastered the art. The Taoist proverb puts it well: "By not doing all things are accomplished." The fretful efforts of both the home and the place of business and work provide all sorts of examples of how by simply not doing anything, much more is paradoxically accomplished.

I learned this first from a pediatric nurse. She told me that the way to spoil a child is to do something for the child that the child can do for himself or herself. For example, if you answer questions that other adults ask the child, you may have the job of doing the child's talking from then on. Then later you may wonder why your child is so non-communicative. Or, if you pick up the child's toys rather than to teach the child to do so, you have the task and the child learns helplessness, a form of hazardous laziness. If you provide an adolescent son or daughter with money that relieves them of the responsibility of learning a skill whereby that son or daughter can earn his or her own money, then you may be depriving the offspring of an identity-formation task from which much self-confidence can arise.

Mothers and fathers will tell me of twenty- and thirty-year-old sons and daughters who are of little use to themselves or other people. The parents are desperate to know "what to do for Jane or Joey." The real discipline, the hard thing to accomplish is *not* doing some of the many things already being done.

Maybe you are the member of the family of an alcoholic, especially a wife or a mother. You have a way of "doing many things" for the alcoholic. Each time drinking gets the person in trouble, you rush in to rescue the alcoholic from his poorly advised situation. You "put a cushion" under the alcoholic and deprive him of hitting bottom and learning from his own experience. By not doing some of these things, the discipline would be of more service to the alcoholic than "knocking yourself out" trying to help. Some such situations are those in which you should run like mad when tempted to help!

Workaholics like me whine a song of self-pity about the amount of work we have to do. When we look around us and do a time and motion study on exactly what work we are doing as it corresponds to the job description for which we are being paid, we discover that we are picking up the loose ends of other people's jobs. We are covering for their dereliction. We are helping them to save face. We do the dirty work. They get the credit for it. We do not do work to get credit for it. If we did, we would not be picking up their duties and making up for their chronic failures to function. Harry Stack Sullivan, the eminent psychoanalyst, says that the professional is the person who seeks to benefit those whom he serves, and he expects to get paid for this service. (*The Psychiatric Interview*, New York: W. W. Norton, 1954, p. 17.) He does not mean that he does *only* that which he gets paid for, but that he actually provides the service for which he is being paid. However, if you are doing another person's work for him, you are depriving him of the privilege of doing what he is being paid for. This is very inconsiderate of you. You leave that person with a sense of weakness that makes you feel strong. In the meantime, you are staying later at night or working on the weekends to get done what you have to do as your own job. The maxim is: When you are overworking, you are doing some other person's job. By not doing something, you will accomplish more for them than by doing something. But to stand idle and do nothing while things go to pieces takes considerable energy on your part. Is it not just easier to go ahead and do it? What is the result of this?

Sooner or later the person whom you are bailing out will turn against you. It is a bad case of casting your pearls before the swine only to have them turn and rend you. Then you will wail your workaholic refrain from having been so rended, "After all that I have done for you, look how you treat me!" In order to exercise your own right to laziness, you can do so in all good conscience if you do not let yourself be snookered into having people obligated to you. You have a profoundly bad conscience when you have taken away another person's potency. The guilt may be obscured by the proud feelings you have, but the disease of the conscience is thereby compounded. The art and discipline of *not doing* prevents anyone from owing you anything. At the same time you prompt in them a sense of strength that is their own. Then they can brag about their own doings. They do not fawn over you for doing things for them that they were perfectly capable of doing themselves. You can revel in their accomplishments. You do not wonder when their idolatry of you is to turn into desecration of you. In *not doing*, all things have been accomplished. You had the day off! You did the things you wanted to do. You did not feel exploited. You could enjoy your laziness in all good conscience. Idling is good for a good conscience.

Your Guilt-ridden Conscience About Laziness

"Yes, but," you say as you have read thus far, "I feel guilty in spite of what you say, even though what you say makes sense in some vague intuitive way. What can I do about this heavy uneasiness, this feeling of guilt? Where did its weight on my conscience come from, and how can I be free of it?"

I say, "Yes, you can do something about your guilt-ridden

conscience. I am glad that you asked what you can do about it. You did not ask why you are like you are. If you had, I would think that maybe you just wanted a tourist's view of the twists and turns of your life history and were loathe to want to do anything at all to change. Grappling with your heritage of accumulated guilt about idleness is no spectator sport. In fact, it is not even a sport. It is jungle warfare against the maze of habitual ways of daily thinking and behaving. Let us hack away at the habits and at the same time appreciate the fact that habits have stubborn roots in our life history. Your bad conscience that keeps you from being lazy in all good conscience has a parental programming. The larger economic deprivations and affluences of the years of the twentieth century have given you either a rearview mirror perspective of the Great Depression or a tyrannical conscience in your ambition-ridden way of life. Several things can be done about such bad consciences. You can shift gears in your way of life for which you will need a survival kit in order to be a genuinely lazy person now in this time. In the order that I have named them here, then, let's think about these topics together.

The Parental Programming of a Bad Conscience

If you think of your whole consciousness as a "computer," the first persons to program your conscience were your parents or those people who took the part of your parents in your life. This does not mean just the early years of your life, although those years are intensely important. The chances are that those same parents are around now telling you similar things when you talk with them by telephone or visit them at their home. They tended to *value* you in terms of your accomplishments in school. You felt that you had their blessing if you worked hard. You felt that you had their disdain or curse if you did not work hard. They may even have contrasted you unfavorably with a brother or sister who was, in their opinion, more productive than you. A strange thing may have happened to you: You had a brother or sister who was the troublemaker, the one who never worked, who was a deadbeat and who caused your parents much grief. Yet, in spite of this, your parents favored that sibling, heaped money upon him, and even expected you to contribute to funds to get that sibling out of jail, out of a drug habit, out of alcoholism, or out of the country. You "knocked yourself out" being a "good person," working hard, achieving much, and making more money. You gave gifts to your parents. You were all stretched out trying to get their approval, a word of appreciation, their blessing for you. Yet, in your guts you felt that you never had that blessing.

Right now—as well as when you were a child—your parents' blessing of you, your achievements, your work, and your station in life has much to do with how good or how bad your conscience functions when you are at play, at rest, goofing off, doing nothing. What do you hear them saying to you when you do not get something done as promised, on time, or ahead of time? "The idle mind is the devil's workshop!" "If all these chores are not done by the time your father gets home, you will get it but good!" "You made a good report card this six weeks, but you could have done better. Why weren't you on the honor roll?" "When I was your age, we had to work from four in the morning to seven, go to school, and then work from four to six. You don't have anything to do but to go to school."

The absence in such messages of appreciation for what you have done is certainly not inspirational. They do not encourage you. They are not blessings. They come more nearly to being "witch messages."

People take different directions in responding to such messages. Some people simply dig in deeper into resentment and frazzle their parents' minds by doing less and less work. They become the people who are afraid to attempt anything lest they fail. They have perfection expected of them. They will settle for nothing less than perfection and wind up doing nothing. Memories and present experiences of parental rejection jam their performance. You are more likely to be a work addict. You will knock yourself out proving that your parents are wrong. You try to please parents who would be satisfied with nothing. You may be chasing the Holy Grail of parental blessing, hoping against hope that someday and in some way those who have not appreciated your efforts will really do so.

Repairing the damage and replacing the parched deprivation of affection for your own sake and your own sake alone may call for the wisdom, encouragement, and acceptance of a good counselor or therapist. But do not leave it to a counselor or therapist alone; you can do something about this yourself. You can "look elsewhere" for that kind of acceptance, appreciation, and affirmation that you never got at home. Not all persons are like your parents. You may assume that *any* person older than you, who has more power than you, who is bigger than you, who has authority over you is *just* like your parents. You may react to them in the same ways you reacted to your parents. For example, employers are often re-enactments of the kind of parents I have described above. They are slave drivers. They make their employees work without adequate equipment. They withhold not only taxes and Social Security; they withhold appreciation, encouragement, and reward for work well done. They, like many parents, function only in terms of their own needs and are devoid of empathy for those who work for them. They reward the more mediocre and penalize the more productive employee. They give the "goodies" to those who "lick up" and "kick down," i.e., lick the boots of superiors and kick the faces of those beneath them in the organizational totem pole. Very soon, if you have such an employer, you may be reacting to him the same way you did to your parents.

The good news is that you do not *have* to do this. You probably have slaved hard enough to have talents and capabilities that others will appreciate. Quit replaying the old parental

tune. Get into a situation where you are genuinely appreciated. You may have some secret delight in being a "good old
Joe or good old Jane" who is last on the list when rewards are
passed out and first on the list when the whole operation is
about to go down the tube, double time is required, and
forced marches with no weekends, no holidays, and no vacations are allowed those who rescue the organization from in-
solvency, public embarrassment, or total collapse. However,
your institution or business is not your home. Your employers
are not your parents. You can quietly start looking for a new
place of work. You can find employers who really appreciate
your past accomplishments, provide tools and assistance for
new achievements, and give you a personal sense of dignity
and worth in your own right.

You need other persons like teachers, employers, and colleagues, to join you as you reassess your own personal sense of
worth. You may, at the bottom of the well, have the uneasy
feeling that you do not really exist except as a worker. If you
are not busy, you are nothing. New people with whom to
work can cause you to feel like somebody's "something" just
for your own sake and your own sake alone. You are in touch
with persons other than employers who can sense strengths in
your effortless graces. For example, you may feel that your
main strengths are in your work and its productivity. They
may feel that your great capacity is that of being loyal and
eliciting loyalty from others. This, they say to you, happens
without your trying or knowing that you are doing so. It is
your *effortless* grace. People around you are eager to do things
that will be of service to you. Yet, in order to feel that you are
somebody, that you exist, you deprive them of the privilege.

Do not wait to get sick to know that you *can* find appreciation from others. If you have had a heart attack, however,
you may know what I am saying here better than I can tell
you. Surprises may be coming to you all over the place when
people lift some of the tasks you have been doing from your
back. They find a great deal of satisfaction in expressing their
affection for and loyalty to you. Yet your bad conscience may

say, "These things I *ought* to be doing myself. I am no good anymore." You are having trouble accepting the grace of others. Come off it!

The Rearview Mirror of a Bad Conscience

As you continue to examine your bad conscience, examine closely the way you look backward all the while life moves forward. You drive forward but are preoccupied with your rearview mirror! Rearview mirrors are for an occasional glance, not a steady stare. I have known but one man who literally drove his car in reverse. One of the colleges I attended was located in a beautiful mountainous area. Professor Stringfield was an unusual man. He drove his car in forward gear when he went home because he lived at the top of a long mountainous road. However, when he returned to the college, which was located in the valley, he always drove in reverse gear. He somehow or other felt that this saved trouble. He felt that he did not have time nor space to turn the car around and let it coast. Half the time he drove either looking in the rearview mirror or with his head out the window looking backward.

Those were the days of the Great Depression of the 1930s. No one had anything. Money was a scarce item. Breadlines fed the unemployed. I worked for ten cents an hour. I felt that I was at the peak of prosperity to make fifty cents an hour. No one felt inferior to his fellow college student because none of them had anything either. Every student was a government subsidized work-grant student. We ate simple food. However, we had the leisure available for the scholarly life. We did not know what a digest or summary of Plato was. We read the whole *Dialogues* in battered copy. We owned no automobiles. We walked where we went or we hitchhiked on trucks. My mother complicated my life for me when I graduated from college. She had saved enough money to buy me a new suit of clothes. I had an old one. Life has been difficult ever since—I have had to *decide* every morning what to wear! Professor Stringfield drove his car backward half the time! He looked backward a lot.

The poverty of the Great Depression left rearview mirror habits in many people's consciences. The memory of the hard times of the Depression years may make you live life now like Professor Stringfield drove his car: staring backward half the time. This is a strange and hazardous way both to drive a car and to live a life. You and I drive ourselves with a Depression-born, backward-looking conscience. If you do not work every minute, save every penny, do without everything except what is really necessary, you will "wind up" in another Depression and have to beg and steal for food. You are conscience-stricken if you are not working like mad, saving your money, being sure that all the bills are paid, and "laying aside for a rainy day."

If you are in the 55–60 age group, you may be working without days off, refusing vacations for more pay, adding moonlighting opportunities to your efforts, and building four or five tax-sheltered deferred income plans to assure that you will not be slaves of Social Security, especially if it goes bankrupt. All the while you are looking back over your shoulder and getting your directions from a bad conscience that was scored and scarred, and now scares you into ceaseless effort. You cannot rest, take leisure, loaf, or exercise your right to laziness because of the rearmirror view of life that guides your driving of yourself.

The Tyranny of an Ambition-ridden Conscience

Not all modern work addicts react in the penny-pinching, look-ahead, prepare-for-the-worst Noah's Ark syndrome I have just described. You may be one of those people who will push the economy for everything it's worth in credit. You do not feel natural unless you are head over heels in debt. You live beyond your means with credit cards, with the marks of affluence that erase your fears that you will ever be anything but wealthy. You may handle much of other people's money in your business. Only a modest wealth, however, is your own. If you are the head of a public institution or a philanthropic, educational, or religious institution, you are likely to have the illusion that the money that other people donate to the agency is yours. You have a champagne appetite but a beer pocketbook. In order to keep the cash flow going to meet the monthly payments, you add more and more work to your day, week, month, and year. As a result, the reverse effect of the deprivation of the Great Depression is the tyranny of "blind ambition" in your bad conscience: You have vowed never to *appear* poor again. You have sworn never to be powerless again. You may own three expensive sports cars and not be able to pay for medical insurance. You are helpless to curb your desire for things and power. Illness, marriage conflict, and business failures may bring you face to face with the way your ambition-ridden conscience works. Some people say, "Let your conscience be your guide." The real question is, Are you living according to a conscience that you yourself have taken executive control in programming, or do you have a conscience that has been whittled and sandpapered by the external "brain washings" of people trying to sell something to you whether you need it or not. Have they appealed to your vanity rather than your good judgment? You can draw the line on your own ambitions and hold it. The result is the renewed power to rest, let things pass, and laugh at the slavery of an inordinate ambition.

You may ask, "Where did this tyranny come from?" You may have been born and reared in abject poverty. Your parents may have suffered severely from oppression by the tenant-farm system, the racial-segregation system, the mining system, the migrant-laborer system, the cotton-mill system, or the ecclesiastical systems that often make unwilling beggars out of ministers and their children. You swore that you would never let that happen to you. Your anger, sometimes bordering on violent rage, literally got behind a brilliant intelligence and an uncanny survival ability to turn poverty into wealth, power, and control over the people around you. Your parents were not the programmers; the system that they allowed to push them into the mud everytime they raised their heads up programmed your conscience. You helplessly watched but quietly resolved that it would never happen to you.

The system of oppression was not the only powerful influence on your development of a tyrannical conscience of ambition-riddenness. The American social-class system that tends to measure the worth of a person by symbols of "having arrived," of "having succeeded," of "having it made" adds fuel to the fire of your burning ambition. Having an education is not enough. You must have it from a "name" school, a name that can be dropped at "show-and-tell" times like cocktail parties, in introduction data to be handed to people who introduce you at a gathering, etc. Having an adequate income is not enough. You must have an income from a prestigious place of work. The local scrap-iron dealer may have a fabulous income. Who wants to be a junk dealer, especially a "local" one? Being on a hospital staff as a physician is not enough. To be on *the* prestigious hospital is the only kind of medicine worthy of the name. Having a home in a reputable neighborhood is not enough. Having a home in a "name" location where all the "best" families live is the goal. Belonging to a club where swimming, tennis, golf, and dining facilities are comfortable, pleasant, and adequate does not satisfy. You must belong to the club that is the most difficult to get in, most exclusive, and in which all of the persons who are the best "contacts" cease to be a luxury and become a necessity.

The American social-class system does not have such power by accident. The programming of what you and I want by the media of television, radio, newspaper, etc., both forthrightly and subliminally, form this set of "oughts" in our consciences. They shape our judgment to want what we did not know we wanted until they kept telling us that we wanted it. Then we begin to believe them. A furniture company's advertisement says: "The name on our truck in your driveway lets your new neighbors know that you belong." The cost of an automobile today is much higher than the first new car I bought in 1946 for $895. Much of that cost is because of inflation. However, that car did not have steel radial tires, air conditioning, automatic transmission, power steering, electric window lifters, electric locking device, cruise control, and rear-window defrosters. The non-glare rearview mirror was its only status item. Now, all of the items I have named are not "status items." They are "necessities." The shift from status item of luxury to standard item of necessity into our decision making as to what we need is produced by an unremitted indoctrination by the media.

You can do something about your ambition-ridden conscience. The best place to start is to ignore the latest "status item." If you give in, it will become a necessity. I wish for you that you will have the ambition to become the kind of person who will cause people to judge what you have by you yourself and not make up their minds as to who you are and what kind of person you are by what you have. Please get with it now! Avoid the loneliness of which Fyodor Dostoyevsky wrote: "Why, the isolation that prevails everywhere, above all in our age—it has not fully developed, it has not reached its limit yet. For every one strives to keep his individuality as apart as possible, wishes to secure the greatest possible fullness of life for himself; but meantime all his efforts result not in attaining fullness of life but self-destruction, for instead of self-realisation he ends by arriving at complete solitude. All mankind in our age have split up into units, they all keep apart, each in his own groove; each one holds aloof, hides himself and hides what he has, from the rest, and he ends by being repelled by others and repelling them. He heaps up riches by himself and thinks, 'how strong I am now and how secure,' and in his madness he does not understand that the more he heaps up, the more he sinks into self-destructive impotence. For he is accustomed to rely upon himself alone and to cut himself off from the whole; he has trained himself not to believe in the help of others, in men and in humanity, and only trembles for fear he should lose his money and the privileges that he has won for himself." (*The Brothers Karamazov*, New York: The Modern Library [n.d.], p. 363.)

Shifting from a Bad Conscience to Laziness in all Good Conscience

You can liken a bad conscience to a defective transmission. I owe this parable—both in terms of dollars and cents and in frustration, wasted time, and frayed temper—to General Motors. We own a 1976 Chevrolet as a family car. At 12,000 miles the warranty expired. At 16,500 miles the transmission expired. It died. I like to use plain language about death. We returned the car to the dealer four times, and the car was in the shop a week at a time each return. The mechanics were superb in their efforts to get the "thing," as they began endearingly to call the transmission, fixed. I sought to give them encouragement, patience, and support. All the while I was starting a consumers' right war with the local Customer Misrepresentative for General Motors. I used my frustration, anger, and roaring feelings of injustice upon the paper shufflers. They finally paid for the parts and I paid for the labor. It cost me three hundred dollars at that. What a hassle!

The final complaint I brought to the mechanics, however, was easily fixed. It took about a half hour. I waited for the car while they did so. The gears would not shift. The linkages were not connected properly. Consequently, I could not use the reverse gear at all. I could not shift except into high gear. I could run and not be towed in if I aimed the car in the right direction and drove in high gear. What a parable of the situation of the work addict! Always in high gear, unable to shift speeds, just hoping to be going in the right direction! I wish my insistence on staying in the same gear of work-work-work could be "fixed" in as short a time and with the skill that the remarkable mechanics fixed the family car. Maybe the whole issue is less serious, at this point of our understanding a bad conscience that deprives us of the right to laziness, than we had thought. Learn to shift to a good conscience about laziness.

Being lazy with all good conscience calls for shifting your conscience into a "gear" of permission to do so with good feelings about yourself and the world. Several functional necessities enable you to be lazy in all good conscience.

As I have indicated, you may have a bad conscience when its gears will not shift. You are stuck in full speed. Your only control is the accelerator. You may think that the only solution is to increase the speed. You use more and more energy. You become exhausted. Then you throw yourself out of gear, stop, and feel guilty because you are doing nothing. Nena O'Neill and George O'Neill talk about finding security in a changing world in their book *Shifting Gears.* (New York: Avon Books, 1974, p. 70.) They say that the process usually takes place in some kind of crisis that "challenges our assumptive state, the external and internal givens of our lives. The transition between one phase of adulthood and another can present such a crisis—so can marriage, the birth of a child, or the death of a loved one. But in other cases, the shifting of gears does not require that you move on to a new assumptive state. You simply rearrange the components of the existing one. It is the difference between moving from one house to another and simply redecorating the one we have.

The O'Neills' book is of great assistance to you as you learn to shift the gears of your life into a state of earned laziness in all good conscience. I would like to take you on a different journey. I use "shifting gears" as a parable of your moving into the right to laziness without the tyranny of a bad conscience. The operation of your life with a good conscience involves several sources of energy, the stuff of which life itself is both made and maintained. The energy supply of life is spent and stored. Energy is neither created nor destroyed. It consists of two kinds: kinetic energy—moving energy—and potential energy—stored energy. Work involves *moving* energy. Rest, leisure, earned laziness involves storing energy. The systole and diastole action of the heart represent the basic necessity of the storing and potentiating of energy as well as the using and exertion of energy. Unless you permit yourself to store energy as well as push yourself to move energy to take place, you disturb the nature of life itself. That is the result of having a bad conscience that will not let you shift gears from kinetic energy to potential energy, from moving energy to stored energy. Renewal does not take place.

In the course of your life, you have several budgets. They all represent energy in one form or another. You have time. You have money. You have stimulating relationships nourished by communication. You have personal power needs, i.e., for prestige. These budgets keep life meaningful. Do you know, however, *which* budget is most depleted? The depleted budget *controls* all the other budgets. You may be working feverishly to get more money. Yet that budget may be your most fully stored budget. Where is your budget of greatest scarcity? Shift to storing, stocking, and supplying it. The chances are that you need rest and renewal worse than you need money, prestige, or anything else. The budget of rest for storing energy is often imperialized by the money budget. So much so is this that we consider the word "budget" to mean money. You are stuck in the money gear. A close re-examination of your conscience reveals that you have become set in your ways to value money above everything else. Many national estimates indicate that workers prefer to have more money to having more time free, as has been said earlier.

Money is closely tied to prestige needs. Your conscience tells you that you are worthy in terms of the amount of money you make, the kinds of symbols of affluence you can show. "Conspicuous" consumption, not poverty, makes your conscience prey to fatigue. You really do not die from overwork but from insatiable ego needs. Once you shift out of the gear of prestige into even a "reverse snobbery" of being known best by the things you do not have, which are usually the perquisites of people "in your position," the more time and energy you have for being free of the treadmill of debt, overwork, and spending of money. A shift out of this gear will make it a lot easier to exercise your right to laziness "in all good conscience."

I have been trying to convey that a good conscience permits you to rest, to be lazy when you are tired from your labor. It is unnecessary for you to feel guilty when you have a day off, when you are letting your mental well-being catch up with itself from the hassles of the past week, or when you catch yourself feeling like a parasite when you are loafing on your own time. Such feelings of guilt are unnecessary. I recall a father bringing his seven-year-old daughter to me asking me to be of help to her. While the child waited with her mother outside, I asked the father, "What do you think is wrong with your daughter?" He said, "She has an unnecessary conscience." I asked what he meant by an unnecessary conscience. He said that his daughter would go to school. The teacher would ask her to go to the blackboard. The little girl would complete her work and inadvertently put the chalk in her pocket. When she got home and found it, she would be overwhelmed with fear and shame. She would be afraid that the teacher would accuse her of stealing the chalk. She felt that she had indeed stolen the chalk and was afraid to go back to school for fear the teacher would catch her at it. After telling this story, the father said, "Don't you think that is an unnecessary conscience?" Take an inventory of the things you are doing. A half of them are highly worthy things to be doing. A fourth of them are unnecessary. The other fourth are counter-productive and probably would do more if left undone.

It is indeed an unnecessary conscience. When it comes to working, you may have an unnecessary conscience. You cannot be lazy in all good conscience. You have more conscience than you need. Such a conscience makes you a slave. You are in bondage to your own unnecessary sense of guilt, shame, and worthlessness if you are not working. Why not overhaul that conscience and get rid of all the phony additives, the unnecessary junk that has accumulated through the years. Start feeling good about being lazy in all good conscience!

A Lazy Person's Survival Kit

In order that you may do what I have been urging that you do, you will need a pattern for being sure that your daily, weekly, monthly, and annual quotient of laziness is rightfully yours. Estimates indicate that the average worker in America has 122 days off (including weekends) from work in a given year. Everyone you know has his or her little list of names of people to get to do this, that, and the other. When they ask, you will promise anything as long as it is a week away in time. Then you start to draw on your surplus time for some honest-to-goodness laziness. You find that you are bankrupt. I suggest the following set of questions for taking an inventory, for creating more laziness time, and for doing so with a free sense of happiness and abandon. Check yourself out by this check list. Then take the post-test on laziness at the conclusion of this chapter. I promised it at the beginning of this book.

1. WHAT KIND OF PROMISES HAVE YOU MADE IN THE LAST YEAR?

All your life you have heard that promises kept are good. It is the promises you keep that help you sleep. It is the promises you break that keep you awake. But let me say to you that some of them are poorly made and need to be broken.

Take a pad and list all the promises you have made. Rank the promises according to the way they fall either at the center of your life purposes, toward the circumference, at the periphery, or have nothing at all to do with your life purpose. The further from the center you get, the poorer judgment went into making the promise. In blunter language, the further from the center of your life purpose, the dumber the promise is. You are too soon old and too late smart.

Get in touch with the people to whom you have made foolish promises. Cancel the engagement, the deadline, or the plan. They will think all the more of you if you cancel the thing before the situation is right at hand. As I suggest this, you are already asking, "What will I tell them? How can I do that? I can't just say that without giving a good reason." Now that you are asking this question, move on to the second item on this check list.

2. ALWAYS HAVE A PERFECT EXCUSE FOR EVERYTHING

You have also heard it said, "An excuse is a neglect of duty." I suggest that an excuse that has validity helps you to define clearly what your duty is and is not. You need a perfect excuse for everything in order to exercise your right to laziness in all good conscience.

These excuses change from time to time, situation to situation, and person to person. For example, I am writing a book now. I have a deadline to meet. If someone calls on the phone in the next hour, I can say no to their request by simply saying, "I am sorry. I can't do that. I have a book deadline breathing down my neck." If I want to cancel an engagement that is four months off, I can say, "When I made that engagement with you, I had no way of knowing that I would have a book deadline on the same day. Will you let me off the hook this time?" Four months away is as vague to them as it is to you or me. They do not feel treated unjustly by having been given such a perfect excuse. Another perfect excuse may be that you have a new baby coming at or about that time. Now, I ask you, what hard-hearted person could feel badly toward you with an excuse that perfect? An outstanding excuse would be to say that you did not realize that your oldest daughter was going to get married at the time you made the appointment. She surprised all of you with her plans. Some scrooge of a task master will say, "You are bound to your obligation to me, nevertheless." If so, just pause on the telephone in a long, stunned silence until he asks if you are still on the line. Wait a few seconds and say, "I have finally gotten my breath back. Your response to my daughter's wedding knocked the breath out of me. Do you have daughters?"

You would be well advised to have a large repertoire of perfect excuses. You find a fiendish glee in lying supinely on your bed while you develop the list. Rotate them. No one excuse can be used repeatedly. Remember, though, you are not just exercising your right to laziness. You are a creatively lazy person! You will discover some ego-shattering reversals in your attempts to remand old, foolishly given promises: Some of these people are going to be relieved themselves. I recall a man calling me last summer to cancel a promise that he had made me. He was very nervous and apologetic. What he did not know was that I was contemplating using my most recent perfect excuse to cancel myself! I had to reassure him several times that he was doing me a great favor.

3. YOUR SCHEDULE HAS BECOME OVERGROWN: MOW IT!

Since you were baby-fed at specific times, you have been taught to have a set, unchangeable schedule. I say: The thing needs changing more often than the oil in your car. Here are a few ways to do it.

All sorts of strange things have grown up in your schedule when you were not looking. You have been knocking yourself out catching up with last year's promises. You have not recently taken a look at the present and forthcoming year's promises. Do so now. The thing really does need mowing! It needs weeding.

Cut out the trivial stuff. You can decide that a task is trivial this way. Is it tied into your regular, long-term commitments? If it is a "one shot" thing that really has no tie-in with your "on-goingness," the chances are that it can be cut down and weeded out. Again, is it a futile effort? Has this organization been arguing about the same problems for the last fifteen years and now they want you to join their "Board of Advisors"? Check around. Ask the board member who resigned what the situation is. The chances are that you will be a "rubber stamp" member to fill an unexpired vacancy on the board to make their stationery look good. Of course, not all boards are like this. But enough of them are so that I hope this paragraph will make some agency executive angry enough to re-examine his or her use of the board.

Cut out the assignments that bore you to death. Assignments like this take more energy than others. You will be counting the hours until the "thing is over." Many "forced marches" are boring. Yet not all such marches are forced. You *chose* to be there. You can choose not to be there. A boring assignment is "quarry slave" work. Put in its place a form of leisurely laziness that brings you pleasure and enables you to bring pleasure to others, especially the people who are intensely important to you. You have a right to extinguish boredom from your life in meaningful ways of creative laziness.

4. GIVE FIRST PLACE TO NON-REPETITIVE EVENTS IN YOUR LIFE HISTORY

You have always said to yourself, "My duty at work comes first." That leads to dullness. Insist that celebrations of non-repetitive events transcend this priority. *Cut out the meetings you attend often enough* to see whether you feel deprived in not attending, or more than one person notices that you were not there. Then rethink your meeting schedules.

The day my son went to war, thankfully, was a non-repetitive event. The day he returned safely was non-repetitive. The day your first-born child goes to school for the first time is non-repetitive. Any birthday or anniversary is non-repetitive. You give such events precedence over and cancel all other commitments insofar as is humanly possible. Anyone who does not understand your actions in putting work aside for celebration, mourning, reunion, farewells, etc. needs to be taken lightly anyway. He is taking himself too seriously. You may choose to get someone to cover your services for you if matters of life and death, emergency, etc. are at stake. Yet you yourself may have a gnawing conscience that condemns you for doing so. Give your gnawing conscience a bone to gnaw on. Take the day or the week for the event that will not pass this way again.

5. DO WHAT YOU UNIQUELY CAN DO

You have always heard that no task is too lowly for you to do. You may not have heard that you are responsible to do what is best done by you.

Recommend others for that which either they uniquely can do or for that which any number of persons can do and do well. I recall working as a weaver in a towel company. I talked with a brilliant young college student who was home for the summer. He asked me if I intended to continue doing the work of a weaver. I said yes. He said, "That's fine, but anyone can do that. Why don't you find something that only you can do?" That has stuck in my mind for the rest of my life. It is a way of making clear decisions as to the maximum use of our energies. Cutting out other things, recommending · other things for other people, and just plain leaving a lot of things undone gives you more time for exercising your right to laziness with a good conscience. You will have much more leisure if you concentrate on doing that which is uniquely yours to do. You want to demonstrate to those about you that you are not afraid to get your hands dirty, that you can do any task as not being too menial for you. Go ahead and demonstrate it. Yet, if you make that a way of life, you will find them standing around watching you while you do the work. Do the things you are capable of doing that they are not.

This looks at first as if it were an incursion of pride. To the contrary, you will discover yourself doing a lot of things that others are *better* at doing than you are. To admit this is a kind of frank humility. Yesterday a man asked me to go a long distance to consult with his hospital about how to set up a hospital chaplaincy. I *can* do that. It is not my long suit. I am not uniquely capable at it. Instead of accepting his invitation, I warmly urged and encouraged him to get a person who has unique, outstanding ability in chaplaincy administration. I revel in that man's superiority to me in that kind of work. No. You do not necessarily have to be a pride-ridden snob to opt to do that which you can uniquely do. Doing so leaves you time for creative laziness that otherwise would be frittered away while you "go through the motions" of work.

6. LET OTHER PEOPLE DO A FEW THINGS FOR YOU

You have always heard do unto others as you would have them do unto you. But do you give them the chance to do that for you?

If you are a workaholic, you do not with much ease let other people help you. *You* have to be in the helper position, the strong position, the doing position. You have trouble giving up and giving into your own deep needs to depend upon others, to have them do things for you, and to receive as well as give. I suggest that another way to exercise your earned right to laziness is to let other people do some things for you. You might even develop the capacity for gratitude. I recall a student of mine whose feelings were hurt and he was deeply angered because I would not let him take my baggage—which was too heavy for a person with a bad back to carry—from the car to the baggage counter at the airport. I remember with what exhilaration I approached the opportunity to "cover" for my graduate professor by teaching a class for him. It has taken me a considerable while to permit other people to do things for me. The most constant feedback I get from my friends is that they enjoy doing things for me, but I rarely let them do so.

7. QUIT TRYING TOO HARD

Wise persons have said, "Genius is 99 per cent perspiration and 1 per cent inspiration." Have you ever thought that leaving only 1 per cent of your time for reflection, thinking, resting also makes your valiant trying counterproductive?

I recall an Air Force colonel whose task it was to command flight training for new officers. I asked him what it was that cause them to fail most often. He said that it was not that they lacked ability. It was not that they were poorly motivated or lazy. It was not that they were unprepared. They failed most often, he said, because they tried too hard. He pointed out that flying a plane calls for knowing the air currents and *letting* the craft co-operate with them. The officer who was trying too hard tried to do all the flying himself. He tried so hard that he "got in his own way," thereby becoming his own worst enemy.

You can search yourself and identify those times that you messed up because you were straining at the task. You engaged in overkill. You were so edgy to succeed that you countermanded your own best efforts. Football players who are consistently offside are trying so hard that they are penalized. Can you cool it? Can you reduce the length of your day and simplify the number of movements in your task? Can you sleep with more abandon on Sunday nights before a week's work by asking your family and friends to tell you when *they* think you are trying too hard?

8. DARE TO LET THINGS HAPPEN

Wizards in business, professions, etc. say, "Plan ahead. Develop five- or ten-year plans." Then, I would ask, "What about the great events of history that have been entirely unplanned?" A wise Oriental proverb says, "The planned life can only be endured."

Maybe you are one of those persons who has to plan everything. If the plans run amok, you become unglued. You cannot stand not knowing what every move and minute is to be. You hold long meetings to make a labyrinth of plans for the work to be done. Agenda anxiety runs out everybody's ears, fumes out their nostrils, and oozes out their pores.

Do you dare to let a considerable number of things happen? Can you live serendipitously to any extent at all? Serendipity means "letting things happen" more or less fortuitously. One does not pre-program, pre-package, and pre-plan with such vengeance that the spontaneous happenings cannot occur. Great vistas of unprogrammed time permit the unusual to occur. This may look like loafing. It really is! Yet, it is creative loafing. You are free enough to respond to the glowing, lumi-

nescent happenings that occur without plan. Keeping the late
afternoons free for this is an important way of not taking bun-
dles of unfinished work home with you. You leave enough free
time unscheduled at the end of the day that you can "mop up"
the operations rather leisurely. If there is nothing to do, you
can beat the afternoon rush and take a nap. This is better than
feeling that you have to eat food or take too much booze to
pick you up enough to be able to drag home.

I learned about letting things happen when I was in the
fourth grade. My mother worked in the cotton mill as a
weaver all of the time before I left home at thirteen and went
to work on my own. She wanted me to have something to do
when I got home from school and before she got home from
work. She encouraged me to start raising chickens. We got a
couple of hens and a rooster to get things started. The hens
laid eggs and I was told to let them alone and not handle
them. Then the hen began to sit on them to hatch them with
the warmth of her body. After many days the little chicks
began to push their bills through the shells. I became excited
and went into action to help. I pulled some of the shells off.
To my dismay, all my efforts had killed some of the young
chickens trying to hatch. My mother was very patient with
me. She taught me that I should leave them alone and wait on
the warmth and attention of the mother hen to bring the little
ones to hatch. Some things do not need to be planned. A better plan than you can devise is already in action.

You may be like a child in your awareness of time, process,
and growth. The granddaughter of a friend of mine said to
him, "Grandpa, I want this done now, right in the middle of
now!" Or, you and I may be also like our oldest son when he
was four who asked for something. I replied, "Just wait
awhile. It will happen just when you are least expecting it."
He went about his play for about ten minutes and returned
and said, "Daddy, I am least expecting it now!"

9. DO IT NOW, LOAF LATER

I once knew a wholesale lumberman who taught me how to
have time to tell stories, drink coffee, rest in the shade, or

sleep. He said that when he arrived at the office desk in the morning, he would not lay a piece of paper down until he had made a decision that got it off his desk. He did it right then. He did not let it pile up. He threw away what needed throwing away. He researched what needed researching for making a decision. He gave an answer to what needed answering. He seemed to have the answer to procrastination. He did not spin his wheels idling in indecision.

You may say, "Well, I need time to think about such decisions." His answer would be, "Your first careful response is probably your most honest and accurate one." The capacity to trust your own judgment is a secret of decision making that saves you time needed for your own personal enjoyment of your free time. The person who makes decisions the way my lumberman friend did is rarely the one who has his desk at home cluttered with piles of unattended matters. Such piles of stuff have a way of keeping you awake, cutting your initiative, and robbing you of the enjoyment of your lazy times. If you do it now, you can loaf later.

10. DO A DISAPPEARING ACT

Your "image," you have always heard, depends on your visibility. But I insist that if people can't find you, they can't work you. Granted that you leave your service covered by responsible people, you have every right to go *incommunicado* for a space of time. One of the ways I do this is to visit my sons at their homes. I cannot be reached by anyone when I am there. My wife alone knows where I am. Calling at the office, people are asked to leave a message. Calling at home, they are asked the same thing. As I have said earlier in this book, going to a different part of my own city enables me to do a "disappearing act." You, too, have a right to do this. In the fret and confusion of stress situations in the job, I have found that to get in my car and drive outside the city to small, interesting villages in the open country is a vast kind of doing nothing in particular that I enjoy. The important factor is that no one can reach me. I encourage you to do similar things. Your survival as a person of good judgment is at stake. Your judgment depreciates in its effectiveness after a sensory overload of warring opinions of upset people. Your very human spirit needs "combing out" as surely as does your hair.

11. GET IN TOUCH WITH YOUR BODY BEFORE YOUR BODY GETS IN TOUCH WITH YOU

You have heard that we should ignore the demands of the flesh. But the flesh is the messenger of our limitations. Therefore, I suggest you stay in attentive touch with your body.

The signals of your body let you know that the storing of energy is sorely lacking. Notice the depth of your breathing. If it is shallow, anxiety is taking oxygen from your blood stream. Notice your weight. If you are gaining weight, is there a possibility that you are substituting food for rest and relaxation? Is there a focus of pain anywhere? If so, you might read this as the need for a diversion before a set of specific symptoms appears that will not take no for an answer. Notice your throat. If it is dry and husky, you might ask if you have pushed yourself to the point of dehydration. A water-fountain break is in order. A headache, an uneasy stomach, and a revulsion for some kinds of foods and drink may forewarn your laying yourself wide open for an infection. Listen to your body before your body has to get authoritarian with you and knock you down.

12. STAY DOWN FOR THE COUNT OF NINE

You have lived according to the maxim, "Don't use sickness as a means of avoiding work. Keep on keeping on." Better wisdom says, "Stay down for the count of nine when illness knocks you down."

Suppose you have ignored all the signals of your body and you do indeed get sick. Stay down for the count of nine. Boxers know that this is permissible. It does not cost anymore. When illness knocks you out of work, your first heroic effort is to get back up before nature has had any opportunity to heal the body. You pop right back up. Then you take another nose dive and have to stay down for a week or ten days. If, in the first place, you had stayed down for at least seventy-two hours —preferably ninety-six—you probably would have felt better, gotten well more certainly, and not have had a relapse. As long as you are down, why not enjoy a good novel? Why not use this as a "perfect excuse for everything"? But are you one of those who feels that you not only do not have a right to laziness; you do not have the right to be sick? Who do you think you are? Is your disembodied spirit not subject to the laws of health? Are you exempt from being personally responsible for accepting the limits of your human body? You think you might be able to jump off a tall building and not even bruise your heel or break a leg? Maybe you are a god, not a human!

13. QUIT RUNNING FROM YOUR LONELINESS

You have always heard that when you are lonely, you should get busy and do a lot of things; you should invite some friends in for a party. You should escape loneliness. Overwork is one way of running from loneliness. I suggest that for your own survival you come to terms with your loneliness rather than run from it. Look it straight in the face and deal with it creatively. Arnold Toynbee said that he is a confessed work addict. He says that the source of his work addiction is his fear of loneliness. I would say as another confessed workaholic that this is one of the most compelling reasons for my own work addiction. This loneliness is not because of the lack of a loving family; I could not hold them responsible for it. It is not due to the lack of friends. It is not due to uninspiring work. The loneliness does not come from any source except from the depths of my being as a built-in aversion to boredom, a restless curiosity, and a sense of not wanting to impose my more abstract thinking processes upon other people. Yet it is a kind of loneliness that I run from, too. I must quit it and you must quit it.

Carl Sandburg spoke most eloquently of loneliness in an interview with Ralph McGill in 1966. He and McGill were walking about Glassy Mountain, near Sandburg's home. He said to McGill: "I often walk here to be alone. Loneliness is an essential part of a man's life and sometimes he must seek it out. I sit here and I look out at the silent hills and I say, 'Who are you, Carl? Where are you going? What about yourself, Carl?'

"You know, one of the biggest jobs a person has is to learn how to live with loneliness. Too many persons allow loneliness to take them over. It is necessary to have within oneself the ability to use loneliness. Time is the coin of life. You spend it. Do not let others spend it for you."

When you keep pushing more and more work into the lonely spots of your life, you are ordinarily letting others spend time for you. Do it yourself and quit running from your loneliness. The rest you get will be healing.

14. LET THE RATS WIN THE RAT RACE OF COMPETITION

You have heard persons like Andrew Carnegie say that "the law of competition may be sometimes hard for the individual, [but] it is best for the race, because it insures the survival of the fittest in every department." (*The Gospel of Wealth,* 1889. Quoted in *Great Quotations,* compiled by George Seldes, Secaucas, N.J.: Lyle Stuart Inc., 1966, p. 143.) But competition, I would suggest, is calculated to multiply stress in human life, depersonalize the best quality of work, and deny persons the right to leisure, the ability to learn leisure. Three years ago one of my colleagues said to me, "Let's keep the rat race from keeping us apart." As I occasionally see him racing from one place to another as I do the same thing, I remember that neither he nor I have been very successful at our vow. Many of the most fretful and least productive "overwork and never rest" tours of duty you and I have crawled home from in total exhaustion were efforts to get ahead, keep ahead, or to keep abreast of our individual or corporate competitors. Much of the waste of time, energy, money, and life comes about by reduplicating, copying, and mimicking the original work of others. Why not let them kill each other off without breakneck competition yourself? You will find plenty of people who will collaborate with you or be at leisure with you.

In conclusion, let me quote Walt Whitman: "Go loaf and invite me." And I can promise you if we do so, we will be in the majority!

These fourteen points for inventory will let you know whether you are indeed storing potential energy and moving kinetic energy. They will let you know rather precisely how bankrupt your laziness account is. As you assess the following continuum questionnaire, you will know how far below the level of your true humanity you are by the number of each continuum you check. You can return to this continuum test later and recheck your progress.

A Lazy Person's
Post-test Guide

Comparing your answers for the following questions to the Pre-test that you took at the beginning of the book, please note your progress or lack of it, as you have learned to "make laziness work." Check your score three months from this date and chart your progress on a continuum.

1. HAVE YOU DECIDED UPON A "POSITIVE ADDICTION" YET?

    a) I'm not sure that a "positive addiction" will work for me.
    b) I'm considering several "positive addictions."
    c) I'm giving one alternative a trial period.
    d) My "positive" addiction" has been so rewarding, that I'm looking for ways to enhance it.

2. HAVE YOU DROPPED OUT OF SIGHT LATELY?

    a) I'm not convinced that it's good for me to "escape."
    b) I'm looking for places to hide, but haven't found one yet.
    c) I've planned a trip and have set the date.
    d) I've been "out of sight" for a week and it's great!

3. WHERE DO YOU RATE YOURSELF ON THE SCALE DEFINING "RESPITE FROM WORK"?

$$-10 \; -9 \; -8 \; -7 \; -6 \; -5 \; -4 \; -3 \; -2 \; -1$$
$$0 \; +1 \; +2 \; +3 \; +4 \; +5 \; +6 \; +7 \; +8 \; +9 \; +10$$

4. BY PRESCRIPTION, HAVE YOU DECIDED WHAT YOUR MAXIMUM AND MINIMUM DOSAGE OF LAZINESS ARE?

   a) I still have no idea how much laziness is right for me.
   b) I'm trying different dosages each week until I find an appropriate one.
   c) I've prescribed a specific dosage of laziness and will adhere to it for one month.
   d) The laziness in my life now fits like a glove!

5. HAVE YOU DECIDED WHOSE JOB YOU ARE CONSISTENTLY DOING AND TAKEN STEPS TO STOP IT?

   a) As soon as I finish my secretary's typing, I'll confront the problem.
   b) I've identified whose job I've been usurping, but don't, as yet, have a plan for stopping.
   c) I've made arrangements to give myself a different job description.
   d) Last week one of my associates helped me on a difficult assignment. We both loved the experience!

6. HAVE YOU EXAMINED THE ANGER UNDER YOUR PROCRASTINATION AND DECIDED TO "DO THINGS NOW"?

   a) My procrastination is not an expression of anger. I'm just behind.
   b) I understand what causes my procrastination and will do something about it—as soon as I can get around to it.

c) I finally caught up on three of the five tasks I've been putting off.

d) Procrastination is not half as good an expression of anger as—subtle screaming!

7. HAVE YOU FACED UP TO YOUR FEARS OF FAILURE AS WELL AS YOUR NEED FOR COURAGE TO BE LAZY IN ALL GOOD CONSCIENCE?

a) I'm still a failure.

b) Despite the fact that I'm still afraid of failing, I've mustered up enough courage to try.

c) Failing doesn't frighten me any longer, but I wouldn't call myself "courageous."

d) My lazy soul has got the best conscience in town!

8. HAVE YOU MADE SPECIFIC PLANS FOR A VACATION OF AS MUCH AS ONE WEEK, AS WELL AS SEVERAL TWO-DAY VACATIONS?

a) I've still got two weeks left over from last year.

b) I'm thinking about when and where I should take my vacation.

c) I've been taking mini-vacations on the job and am planning a two-week vacation.

d) My week in Hawaii was great—and I can't wait to go again!

9. HAVE YOU ARRANGED A SYSTEM OF PRIORITIES FOR SAYING "NO" TO DEMANDS LAID ON YOU?

a) Saying "No" hurts people. I just can't!

b) I've picked out two solicitors of my time and have premeditated my "No" for them.

c) I've started to say "No" to unreasonable and unrealistic

requests. I'm procrastinating less and accomplishing more.

d) Knowing my priorities has eliminated a lot of wasted time and increased my efficiency.

10. WHAT IS YOUR REPERTOIRE OF PERFECT EXCUSES TO REFUSE TO WORK MORE? WRITE THE THREE BEST ONES HERE.

a) _____

b) _____

c) _____

11. HAVE YOU LEARNED TO ENJOY BEING ALONE?

a) Of course—just as long as being "alone" doesn't mean being by myself!

b) I'm rearranging my schedule, so that I have a half-hour by myself every day.

c) I was afraid of loneliness, but no longer am.

d) I know it's overused, but I'm my own best friend.